SCIENCE AND SINGING

SCIENCE
AND SINGING

A CONSIDERATION OF THE CAPABILITIES OF
THE VOCAL CORDS AND THEIR WORK
IN THE ART OF TONE PRODUCTION

BY

ERNEST G. WHITE

WITH 48
PHOTOGRAPHS
AND DIAGRAMS

CRESCENDO PUBLISHING COMPANY
Boston

Standard Book Number 87597-002-8
Library of Congress Card Number 68-59104
Printed in the United States of America
Reprinted by arrangement with J.M.
Dent & Sons Ltd., London,
holders of the copyright.

Affectionately Inscribed

TO MY WIFE,

WHO, AS AMANUENSIS, GAVE ME
MUCH VALUABLE HELP IN THE
PREPARATION OF THIS WORK.

FOREWORD TO THE 1950 EDITION

THIS is the first time an Edition of *Science and Singing* has been issued without the supervision of the author. Ernest G. White died in January 1940, at the age of seventy-seven, fortunate perhaps after so long and full a life never to know the worst years of the war or witness the destruction by flying bomb in June 1944 of the Lewisham house where so much of his life's work was accomplished and whence earlier editions of this book originated.

Science and Singing and the companion volume *Sinus Tone Production* will be the memorials of his originality of mind, his immense thoroughness in the field of study which he discovered concerning the human voice, and his intellectual courage.

Many have been helped in their vocal development by the reading of these books alone. Yet, although White explained his theory and methods as fully and exactly as possible in writing, practical demonstration and tuition are necessary to the full understanding and effective practice of Sinus Tone Production. To preserve and transmit the knowledge of White's practical methods, to develop and perfect his theory, and with these books to be his memorial, the Ernest George White Society has been founded. The Society has already formed a register of those qualified to teach Sinus Tone Production, and established standards for those who wish to qualify. It now has the honour to sponsor this unrevised reprint of *Science and Singing* in the knowledge that here is the original record, which must be preserved, of one of the really great discoveries affecting human life and happiness.

A. D. HEWLETT, *Honorary Secretary*

The Ernest George White Society,
21 Gower Street, London, W.C.1.

vi

ACKNOWLEDGEMENTS TO THE 1950 EDITION

WITH the publication of this sixth edition of Science and Singing I would like to thank our tutors and all others friends who gave their valuable support to me in the progress of Sinus Tone Production through the few difficult war years following my husband's death.

My grateful appreciation is due to the authorized teachers of the Ernest George White Society and School of Sinus Tone in various parts of the country and abroad and to others who are by their unsparing efforts continuing the successful results in Sinus Tone Production, especially in the remedial work for which there is a great demand at home and in other countries.

E. J. WHITE, *Director of Studies*

St. Monica,
East Chinnock, near Yeovil.

4th January, 1950

PREFACE TO THE SECOND EDITION

IN OFFERING this enlarged edition of *Science and Singing* for the acceptance of the public, under the title of *The Voice Beautiful*, I do so with a keen sense of appreciation of much kindness which I have received from those who have studied the first edition. I am fully aware that my views on the art of singing are in distinct opposition to the theories which have hitherto been held upon the subject, and also in opposition to *some* of the practical teaching ; but I would say, as Dr. William Harvey said in dedicating his famous book. *An Anatomical Disquisition on the Motion of the Heart and Blood in Animals,* ' all we know is still infinitely less than all that remains unknown. And then . . . . the studious and good never think it unworthy of them to change their opinion if truth and undoubted demonstration require them so to do ; nor do they deem it discreditable to desert error, though sanctioned by the highest antiquity ; for they know full well that to err, to be deceived, is human ; that many things are discovered by accident, and that many may be learned indifferently from any quarter, by an old man from a youth, by a person of understanding from one of inferior capacity. .... I avow myself the partisan of truth alone ; and I can indeed say that I have used all my endeavours, bestowed all my pains, on an attempt to produce something that should be agreeable to the good, profitable to the learned, and useful to letters.'

Most earnestly do I trust that this enlarged edition of *Science and Singing* will be accepted in the same spirit in which it is offered, namely, a keen desire for the advancement of our art and a sincere wish to be useful to my fellow creatures.

Years ago I used sometimes to wonder if it were possible that my theories could be wrong, but when success after success kept on following in quick succession, my fears grew less and my hopes grew stronger, until I can now say with Sir William Crookes : 'Hopefulness has merged into certainty'—my doubts have vanished. Thus have I proved the correctness of the thought expressed by Sir Francis Bacon : 'If a man will begin with certainties, he shall end in doubt ; but if he will be content to begin with doubts, he shall end in certainties '.

Prentice Mulford, in his essay on *The Gift of Understanding* speaks of ' the constructive force of new. invention, which shall find out by the so-called trivial, despised things of to-day new powers in Nature and new powers in Man, which every man shall find it possible to use, and the wonder then will be that we did not discover it at all before '. The aptness of such language to the present volume will be self-evident to the reader when its contents have been thoughtfully assimilated.

ERNEST G. WHITE

17 *Cavendish Square,*
   London, W.1.
    And 5, Marlborough Road,
     Lewisham, London, S.E.13

1918

FOREWORD TO THE 1938 EDITION

As is so often the case in Research work, results far exceeding the expectation even of the worker have been produced during the course of Mr. White's nearly forty years study of Voice Production along his own original lines.

To all those who have been willing to listen to or read about Mr. White's methods, based on his system of Sinus Tone Production, has come intense interest and, in an ever-growing number of cases, conviction.

Thus it is that enquiries, either by post or in person, have come from the uttermost parts of the earth.

This is not strange when the practical results of his work are considered ; these applied, in the first place, to the purely artistic ideas of vocal work.

In the course of time other results have gradually evolved which are equally or even more successful and important, affecting, as they do, the general health.

Naturally, perhaps, these are the results that hold the chief appeal having proved of such extraordinary benefit to a large group of individuals suffering from what may be generally classified as affections of the Respiratory System.

The possibilties of Mr. White's methods in the prevention and cure of such conditions will, I hope, be generally realized and put into practice in the not-far-distant future.

One can have nothing but the greatest admiration for and sympathy with Mr. White's dogged perseverance and ultimate success achieved in spite of bitter criticism and opposition in the earlier days ; but such is the lot of the pioneer !

REGINALD F. PRICE, M.D., C.M.,

Forest Gate, *Oct.* 1937.

ACKNOWLEDGEMENTS

I AM grateful to many publishers and authors for permission to quote extracts from their works and to use diagrams. Figure 18 is from *Diseases of the Nose and Throat* by Dr. Herbert Tilley, Figure 22 from *Dental Surgery* by Sir John Tomes, Figures 24, 25 and 26 are photographs from specimens in the British Museum, Figure 32 from *Cunningham's Text-Book of Anatomy*.

E. G. W.

CONTENTS

ILLUSTRATIONS

Page

SCIENCE AND SINGING

CHAPTER I

INTRODUCTORY

There is one art of which every man should be master,
the art of reflection.—COLERIDGE.

EVERY month and almost every week, fresh wonders of science and skill are being unfolded and explained to, and for, the benefit of the human race. Many of these discoveries add to the comfort and pleasure of mankind, others do little more than add to his knowledge, at all events at the present moment. Amongst the former may be mentioned the wonders of radio-telephony invented by the Danish scientist, Mr. Valdemar Poulsen, and improved by the late Senator Marconi.

Amongst the latter may be mentioned the marvels of radio-activity as discovered by Dr. Lazarus Barlow, and his co-investigators ; that a calculus taken from the body of a mummy still possessed radio-influence, although it was over 4,000 years old. Also the marvels of life as revealed by the microscope, *e.g.*, those tiny creatures known as ' rotifera ' ; and that eminent scientist, the late Dr. Dallinger, in one of his lectures used to speak of a parasite of a parasite of a parasite ! Surely here is a most extraordinary example of the minuteness of scientific discovery. Charles Darwin said that the brain of an ant was perhaps the most marvellous speck of matter in the universe.

On the other hand, if we think of big matters, that is, of course, big with respect to size, we know with certainty that from the middle of summer to the middle of winter our earth has travelled 280 millions of miles. We know also that this globe is ninety-one millions of miles distant from our sun, yet the distance of the star Alpha Centauri is 200,000 times as much, whilst the lovely Sirius is again at least two or three times as far away. Many other marvels of knowledge and science might be mentioned, but these will suffice.

Therefore, ' considering our present advanced state of culture, and how the Torch of Science has now been brandished and borne about, with more or less effect, for 5,000 years and upwards ; how, in these times especially, not only the Torch still

B   I

burns—and perhaps more fiercely than ever—but innumerable rushlights and sulphur matches, kindled thereat, are also glancing in every direction,'[1] is it not in itself almost a marvel that in this twentieth century the art or science of singing and of speaking (I mean *how*, not what, to speak) is still in a deplorable state of chaos ? Sciences which are intensely abstruse and sometimes of comparatively little practical value can be expressed and spoken of with absolute certainty, whilst the art of speaking, which affects every human being in the world, is still, may I say, in Egyptian darkness. At the inaugural meeting of the Institute of Physics, on 27th April 1921, the Lord President of the council, the Earl of Balfour, caused some amusement by expressing in his speech the opinion that ' the public seldom did know much about the things which most deeply concerned them.'

It has been said, ' When we come to the *method* of training the voice we find not method but pandemonium.' ('Lost Art of Singing,' by M. A. R. Tuker, *Nineteenth Century and After*, August 1903.)

' Pandemonium ' may be a strong word, but it is true, and equally applicable in 1938 as it was in 1903. A short time ago a prominent professor of voice culture informed me that he did ' not admit that there is any principle in the art of singing.' Probably he realized that his piano, his spectacles, his house, were all built on a principle, on a system. Surely the worlds revolve on a principle! But singing—according to this gentleman—has *no* principle. What else then can we expect but ' pandemonium ' ?

Again, Dr. Gordon Holmes, writing on registers, says: ' Further investigations in this direction are much needed. The confusion which prevails in these matters is well illustrated by the statements in some singing methods. Thus, it is represented that in all female voices, contralto and soprano alike, the chest register cannot be carried beyond E. On the other hand, it is allowed that a difference of nearly an octave exists in the upward extent of the various male voices; so that a bass singer cannot usually rise above D from the chest, whilst a tenor may even attain to C♯. The physiological inconsistency, not to say absurdity, of these views need not be dwelt on.'

Another well-known writer and vocal teacher[1] says : ' Almost everything in the material world has been investigated, and its laws found out. Take the curvature of a projectile. Given its weight and velocity, the point at which it will fall is known to a certainty.[2] There is no guesswork, no romance ; here all is sure, all is certain ; but in my profession all is chaos.'

What an endorsement is this of a paragraph which appeared a little time since in a French paper[3] : ' Science solves formidable problems, and is powerless before apparently simple ones.'

But it may be asked, why make such a sweeping assertion ? Is the art of teaching singing in a state of chaos ? I reply, yes, most certainly. Think of the statements which are continually being made with respect to ' nasal resonance,' ' chest production,' ' shock of the glottis,' and various other ideas. We hear of Mr. A's ' method ' of teaching and Mr. B's ' method,' each gentleman declaring that his is the only one that is really correct. In *A Text Book of Human Physiology*, by Landois and Stirling, it is stated : ' The nasal timbre is produced by the soft palate not cutting off the nasal cavity completely, which happens every time a pure vowel is sounded, so that the air in the nasal cavity is thrown into sympathetic vibration. When a vowel is spoken with a nasal timbre, air passes out of the nose and mouth simultaneously, while with a pure vowel sound, it passes out only through the mouth. When sounding a pure vowel (non-nasal), the shutting off of the nasal cavity from the mouth is so complete that it requires an artificial pressure of 30 to 100 mm. of mercury to overcome it.' (Hartmann.) Yet in the musical libel suit Horspool *v.* Cummings held in February 1908, Dr. J. Donelan, who was for some time private assistant to Sir Morell Mackenzie, was asked the following question : ' The amount of nasal resonance which you use in singing is very largely a question of dispute, is it not—some people say the nose is everything, and others that it has nothing to do ? ' In reply he stated : ' Those who say the nose has very little to do are absolutely ignorant of the matter. . . . This is the opinion of all those whose opinion is worth considering.' Sir Milsom Rees

---

[1] The late Mr. Charles Lunn.

[2] As a matter of real fact, other details than those mentioned by Mr. Lunn must be known in order to ensure accuracy in gunnery. But his idea is correct, viz., that mathematical science is able to ensure the utmost precision in dealing with projectiles ; but in the vocal world ' all is chaos.'

[3] *Revue Scientifique*, Paris.

in the same case mentioned, in the course of his evidence, that
' new methods crop up very frequently and die down very rapidly,
too.' He also stated that he doubted the correctness of certain
views held by Sir Morell Mackenzie.

Again, some anatomists are quite convinced that certain muscles,
technically known as the thyro-arytenoid muscles, when brought
into action, have the effect of tightening the vocal cords ; whilst
others on the contrary, hold that their office is to loosen them.

Many other instances could be given showing how authorities
disagree upon the subject and quarrel like two halves of a Seidlitz
powder ; but enough has been said to prove that there is much
work to be done before the art of teaching singing, and perhaps,
one might add, even the art of singing itself, can be considered as
on a really sound basis.

The late Sir Trevor Lawrence, in presiding at the annual
meeting of the Royal Horticultural Society, in 1910, said : ' It is
becoming recognized, although somewhat late in the day, that no
work of importance can well be carried on that does not sufficiently
regard the teaching of science.' Now compare this statement with
another drawn from quite a different source, namely, *The
Philosophy of Voice*, by the late Charles Lunn. This writer
states : ' The intellectual world has not as yet elevated song into
a science, so that it has never been other than a matter of imitation.'

Here on the one hand we have a prominent man of letters
declaring—and quite correctly—that science is absolutely essential
for any and every work of importance, whilst, on the other hand
we have from another expert this equally true declaration that
singing has never yet been a science, but only a matter of imitation.
If both remarks are true—and undoubtedly they are—surely it is
high time that some very real effort was made to put the art of
singing upon a distinctly scientific basis.

Of course we know that there are in our midst very fine and
very clever singers of both sexes, but when we find one medical
voice specialist only, claiming ' an enormous practice ' (Sir J.
Milsom Rees, witness in musical libel case, 13th February 1908)
amongst professional singers, and stating also that most of the
great singers have been to him for advice, surely this fact might
give one cause to stop and consider whether the lines on which
voice training is being carried on are exactly all that they should
be with respect to correctness.

Another point for reflection is the fact that our great artists, as such, are usually very short-lived. The great majority, after being before the public as performers for a few years, then become teachers. Numberless instances of this might be cited, but it will be sufficient to advance three very prominent names, viz., the centenarian, Garcia, and the once famous Polish operatic singers, Jean and Edouard de Reszke. These truths do not by any means exhaust the ideas which might lead a thinking person to pause and consider whether the art of speaking and singing is really quite understood.

It is however, well to remember that music and musical art have ever been very slow in making definite progress, many of the arts having arrived at a high state of proficiency hundreds, and in some cases thousands, of years before the ' divine art.'

The following pages will show that I have dared to think for myself on the thorny subject of voice-production. The ideas are unorthodox, and it is not to be expected that converts to the system will come at first in thousands, but those who do take the trouble to follow the arguments advanced must, I think, be struck with their simplicity, and with the extraordinary manner in which they coincide with the teaching of acoustics. Those who go further and endeavour to put the theories to a practical test, will eventually be astonished at the discovery of powerful tone coupled with sweetness which they have not before experienced either in themselves or their pupils.

The great scientist, Sir W. H. Preece, writes : ' Faraday taught me to regard the facts of nature as always tending towards the simple ; I have invariably found this to be the case.' The statements in this book with regard to singing will be found to conform to the same rule, although they are at variance with the ideas that are to-day accepted as truth.

But we know that Athanasius and Galileo, each in his day, held opinions that were considered heterodox, whilst Christopher Columbus had the greatest difficulty in getting anyone to take an interest in his plans for discovery, because his idea that the earth was globular in form had, so it was stated, such an irreligious tendency ; and this was conclusively proved by his opponents— to their own satisfaction—both from the Pentateuch, the Psalms and the Prophecies, the Gospels, the Epistles, and the writings of the ancient Fathers, St. Chrysostom, St. Augustine and others.

Still, we know now that the earth is not flat, and that night is not produced by the sun hiding himself behind an immense mountain, and I firmly believe that sooner or later it will be seen and acknowledged that the views herein set forth are absolutely correct. If that be so, future generations will have as much respect for our present singing ' methods ' as we have for the science of physiography in pre-Elizabethan days.

It was during the reign of ' good Queen Bess ' that William Harvey—a brave medical reformer and scientist—was born at Folkestone on 1st April 1578. When, after much study and thought, he published in 1628 *An Anatomical Disquisition on the Motion of the Heart and Blood in Animals,* other writers cruelly attacked him, both personally and on account of his work, and sometimes in anything but pleasant language. One who knew Harvey[1] writes thus : ' I have heard him say that after his book of the circulation of the blood came out he fell mightily in his practice, and 'twas believed by the vulgar that he was crack-brained, and all the physicians were against him ; with much ado, at last, in about twenty or thirty years' time, it was received in all the universities in the world.'

Now, although I gladly and thankfully acknowledge the help which the Press has given me in finding much good in my work and praising it accordingly, yet some other writers have spoken with bitter sarcasm and haughty contempt for my doctrines. I will say, as William Harvey wrote to John Riolan[2] : ' Let them go on railing until they are weary, if not ashamed.' Truth will out. That which is right cannot continually be held back by that which is false. Whether I shall be like Harvey and live to see my work accepted over the world as truth, time alone will show.

---

[1] John Aubrey, *Lives and Letters of Eminent Persons*, London, 1813.
[2] Anatomist in the University of Paris.

CHAPTER II

SINUS TONE PRODUCTION

If a thousand old beliefs were ruined in our march to truth,
we must still march on.—Stopford A. Brooke.

' If I may speak of the objects I have had in view since I began
the ascent of my hillock, they are briefly these '[1] : (a) To show
and if possible convince the world in general that the vocal cords,
situated on the top of the windpipe, in what we call our throat
(Figure 1), are not the seat of sound. That is to say, in neither
speech nor song do the vocal cords actually create the tone ; (b)
To show that the whole compass of the human voice is divided
between four sets of sinuses (or cavities) which are found on each
side of the head. These two points contain the whole object of
the present volume.

In my early days, some years were spent in the ' study ' (?) of
singing with a gentleman who was connected with a local conservatoire ; and afterwards I removed to one of our principal
London schools of music, where I experienced the ' training ' of
two other masters, with each of whom I stayed a considerable
time. The total result of all this tuition was that I lost even my
speaking voice.

Some years after this, providentially I met Mr. Hugo Beyer,
and at once saw that from this gentleman I could learn much. It
is due to the foundation that Mr. Beyer laid, followed by my own
close study, thought, and experiment, that the writing of this book
became possible.

The first thing I learnt was *how to act* in order to avoid a throaty
tone, and how many singers there still are who should be taught
the same thing ! That my tutor and I were successful in eradicat-
ing this abomination, is shown by the fact that I never again lost
my voice after my first lesson, although I had previously been
three years under the treatment of doctors and physicians without
getting any permanent relief from my throat troubles.

I learned from Mr. Beyer that it was possible to produce
sound ' above the tongue ' ; and from that lesson I worked and

[1] T. H. Huxley.

7

8   SCIENCE AND SINGING

experimented until I now know and teach'that the vocal cords
are not sound producers at all.

To the great majority of throat doctors and musicians this
statement will come as a surprise, and many will, doubtless,
regard it as ' nonsense,' but the proofs in its favour, both scientific
and practical, are so great, that a mind which is willing to learn
must certainly in future have at least grave doubts whether the
vocal cords themselves are capable of tonality.

There is not the slightest doubt that mankind as a whole
owes a debt of gratitude to Manuel Garcia for the invention of the
laryngoscope, but musically it has had a bad effect, by drawing
the attention of students and singing masters to the study of the
anatomy of the larynx (*i.e.*, the thyroid cartilage popularly known
as ' Adam's apple ' where the vocal cords are enclosed), which,
however interesting it may be in itself, is certainly useless from
a vocal point of view. What person ever sang any better for knowing the position of the cartilages of Wrisberg and Santorini ?
Has anybody's voice improved after learning the action of the
thyro-arytenoid muscles ? Never. In fact, one might go further
than this and say that it is even possible that some may have sung
worse, because the knowledge may have drawn their thoughts in
the wrong direction.

Surely there can be no practical result from the perusal of such
statements as the following, taken from a well-known book on
singing : ' The *superior* laryngeal nerve acts upon the crico-
thyroid muscle and the inferior constrictor muscle. The crico-
thyroid muscle pulls together the thyroid and cricoid cartilage *both
ascending*, and the effect of this action is to tighten the vocal cords,
consequently to raise the pitch. The intrinsic muscle owes its
action to a nerve-energy directed downwards through the
superior laryngeal nerve. Thus much for direction of will or
thinking *downwards* against the initial *automatic* upward pressure.' Surely, I repeat, such statements cannot possibly assist
vocalization.

Again, what practical result can be gained from the following
directions taken from another book ?—' The larynx must rise and
descend unimpeded by the tongue, soft palate and pillars of the
fauces rise and sink, the soft palate always able more or less to
press close to the hard. Strong and elastic contractions imply
very pliable and circumspect relaxation of the same.' I am sorry

for the student who has to try and improve his voice by means of such directions.

By all manner of means, let the vocal student study acoustics, also the anatomy of the head, for each of these subjects will be of great assistance to him in the production of his voice, and in knowing how to use it to the best possible advantage. He should learn—if possible, by examining a skull, but if that be not obtainable, then by means of diagrams—on what an admirable and perfect plan Nature has placed those little voice boxes—or, to give them their correct names, sinuses and air cells—which in my opinion are, with the aid of breath, our sole means of producing vocal tone.

I propose then, in these pages to consider the matter of voice production from two points of view ; the first being that the vocal cords do not produce sound ; the second, to consider if it be possible for them to do so.

Assuming my statement, that the larynx is not the seat of sound, to be correct, we have to determine how sound really is produced.

If the reader will refer to Figure 1, an alternative will be shown. The breath coming up the windpipe passes the larynx at the point V, after which it may be directed out of the mouth as in ordinary breathing, or the mouth may be closed and the breath directed past the pharynx[1] and then through the nose at R, or we can voluntarily direct the breath so that it travels via the sinuses $\mathcal{J}$, P, F, A^1, A^2, and then down the nose, in which case sound is produced. Here is an end to my statement, which is surely simplicity itself. All bother about ' shock of the glottis,' ' false vocal cords,' ' chest voice,' or other matters of the kind has disappeared ; breath is simply directed through the head, and sound is the result.

Of course, plenty of objections may be raised to this simple statement, and a large part of this book will be devoted to the endeavour to dispose of them.

The first objection might be, that mere sound is not necessarily singing, and, even granting that a sound of some sort might be produced in the way explained would it be possible for such a simple arrangement to produce one-and-a-half or two octaves of musical tones ? It may be at once granted, that mere sound is not

[1] The pharynx being membranous cannot very well be shown in Figure 1. Its position is immediately behind the nose and mouth.

necessarily singing, and we will presently examine the physical difference between speech, noise, and singing.

With regard to the question as to whether such a method of producing tone be possible, let the reader imagine himself in a closed room on a very windy day, and he will hear the wind moaning through the keyhole, with the result that half an octave or more of sound is produced. Now, it will not require an elaborate argument to show that the keyhole of a door is not designed or intended as a musical instrument. If then, the greater or less pressure of wind passing through a dead keyhole can produce half an octave of sound, is it a matter for surprise that two octaves should be produced by passing living breath through a live head ?

Two other simple examples of air vibration may be given. The author has on a very windy day stood by a field fenced with iron railings, and heard an ascending scale of five or six notes produced by the air rushing between and past the iron posts. Varying tones may also be obtained from an ordinary oblong metal hot-water bottle. After the hot water has been emptied from the bottle, let the screw be left so that the bottle is not quite closed, and musical sounds will be caused by the outside air rushing into the bottle, and thus filling the partial vacuum which would otherwise be produced by the contraction of the cooling air and vapour.

It is acknowledged that the human voice at its best is, the most charming and delightful of all varieties of tone ; therefore, if the head be the seat of sound, it must of necessity be the one ideal, perfect machine for tone production that can be conceived, and therefore its capabilities are great. Let this matter be well thought over, and it will be seen that the truth of the statement is certainly possible. We therefore may undoubtedly conclude that at all events it is quite possible to produce sounds by the mere passing of breath through the head. Later on it will probably be seen that such an action is more likely to generate tone than that of tightening the vocal cords.

Passing to the argument that mere sound is not necessarily music, the correctness of this is obvious. Let us see then, where is the difference between speech, song, and noise.

A well-known writer,[1] in attempting to explain the difference between speech and song, expresses himself as follows : ' When will professors of singing grasp the fact that nature has ordained

[1] F. J. Crowest.

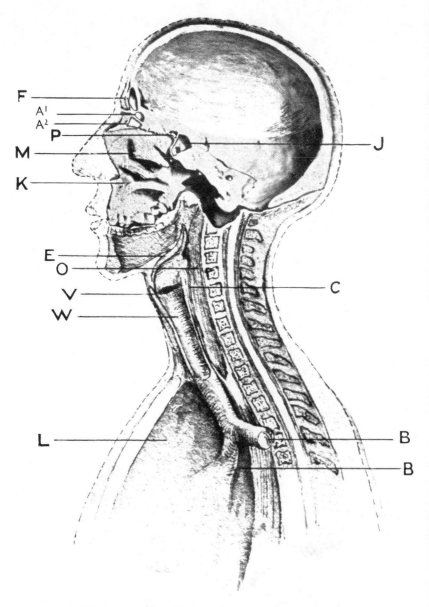

FIGURE 1. THE LUNGS, WINDPIPE, AND SKULL

It is advisable to study this figure by comparing it with Figures 3, 6, 15, 16, 17.

EXPLANATION OF FIGURE I

At and above the chin, the dotted lines represent the complete outline of the head, the remainder is all bone, with the exception of *E*, which is the epiglottis, *i.e.*, a thin leaf-shaped cartilage which assists in closing over the windpipe in the act of swallowing, and so keeps out foreign substances [1]; and the oesophagus or gullet *O*, down which food passes into the stomach. *V* is the situation of the vocal cords. The cords and the various cartilages connected with them are not shown, because a knowledge of them is not here considered of any practical value. They are, however, shown more in detail in Figures 20 and 27, pages 58 and 101. *B B*, right and left bronchi. The right bronchus is shown entering the lung, *L*. *C*, section of cricoid cartilage, which rests upon and forms the top of the windpipe.

A 1. A portion of the lower part of the left frontal sinus.

A 2. Upper part of the infundibulum. The infundibulum is a passage connecting the frontal sinus *F* with the nose. The left frontal sinus is usually the larger of the two, and frequently encroaches beyond the middle line into the right half of the skull. It has done so here.

F. The right frontal sinus, leading down behind *A* 1 *A* 2 by means of the infundibulum into the middle meatus, *i.e.*, the passage marked M, which goes under the middle turbinated bone *N*. *D* is the superior turbinated bone, and just below and underneath it is the superior meatus, that is, the entrance to the posterior ethmoid air cells.

H. Inferior turbinated bone, and immediately below and underneath it is the inferior meatus, where is situated the outlet of the naso-lachrymal canal, which has no bearing upon our subject.

K. The palate bone. The upper surface of this bone forms the floor of the nose, and the underneath surface constitutes the hard palate of the mouth.

J. Sphenoid sinus, where the lowest tones of the voice are formed. The black spot close to the termination of the *J* line is the entrance to the sinus.

P. Part of the posterior ethmoid cells. There is sometimes a connection between these cells and the sphenoid sinus.

W. Trachea or windpipe.

L. Lungs.

The reader who is unacquainted with physiology is advised to continue reading the text, and to give further study to this figure in connection with Figures 2, 3, 6, 14, and 16.

---

[1] It was formerly thought that the epiglottis was alone responsible for keeping the windpipe clear, but from the researches of Professor Anderson Stuart, it would appear probable that other parts of the mechanism assist in making this closure over the windpipe.

the anterior portions of the wonderful vocal cords for the purpose of speech, and that the posterior ends are, broadly, for singing purposes ? '

Now, even if this statement were correct, it could hardly have any practical value, for we certainly have no conscious control over ' the posterior ends ' or the ' anterior portions of the wonderful vocal cords.' This will be further shown on page 60. Such an explanation can, therefore, hardly be regarded as satisfactory.

In reality the difference between speech and song is very simple. It consists in the fact that in singing, the vowel sounds have an exact pitch, and also a definite and quite precise value in length. In speech, both details are indefinite and varying, and the sounds expressed have no relative time value to each other. Let the reader say one word, ' Yes ? ' in an interrogative manner, and then say, ' No ' with a downward inflection, and the rising and falling of the voice in speech will at once be apparent. Here and here only are the differences between song and speech. There is no change whatever in the mechanism used or in the parts affected, and *any* person who can speak is capable of song also, although he may not have a natural aptitude for producing musical sounds.

The drawing master who understands his work, would not send away as hopeless the thoughtful and painstaking pupil who was unable to make a correct curve or a proper copy of a freehand drawing after a few lessons. He would encourage the learner to continue study, and if the work were properly graded, starting with the most simple ideas and working gradually onwards, the pupil would be sure to meet with a certain measure of success, although he might never get within even a reasonable distance of becoming an academician.

So with the study of singing. Some people have a natural gift for song which is denied to others, but let not the less fortunate individual think that the vocal art is therefore an impossibility to him. Should such a one be planted at once in front of a song or study, and told to sing it without further help and directions, then indeed would his chance be a small one, but if the tutor knows how to *assist* his pupil, and lead him along step by step, and perhaps even one note at a time, then, providing always that the learner has a desire to succeed and does not fear the trouble of surmounting difficulties, undoubtedly every person in this world who can speak could sing sufficiently well to ensure that pleasure could be both given and obtained.

Over and over again have I heard it stated that certain people have ' no ear for music,' because they are unable to sing correctly any given melody of a simple nature. The fault in nearly every case has not been in the ear at all, because the person has been only too conscious of the incorrectness of his endeavours. The fault lay in the fact that he was unable to control the voice so as to strike, or produce, the tone that was required. Now in the same way (not of course by the same method) that a child can be led by easily graded curves to control and direct a pencil, and thus produce a satisfactory drawing, so can anyone—provided he can speak—be taught to control and direct the column of air which he breathes so as to produce musical tone, and, eventually, melody. I have proved this several times over.

Let it be distinctly understood that it does not follow that everyone could sing equally well, either with respect to volume or tone.

Leaving speech, let us ascertain the distinction between singing and mere noise. Acoustically the difference consists very largely in the fact that the vibrations which constitute singing are regular, whilst those of noise are irregular in their periodicity. For the present purpose, however, that explanation will not suffice, for we want to know the physical, not the acoustical, difference between the two. The following definition will, I think, answer the purpose. Singing is tone[1] *rightly placed and undisturbed by physical effort and muscular contraction.* It should be more realized that tone is spoilt by muscular effort. This matter will have further attention later on.

What a flood of light is now thrown upon the writing of the old Italian school ' *chi sa respirare sa cantare,*' that is : he who has learned to breathe has learned to sing. How is this explained ? Simply because singing consists solely in passing the breath through the head and not allowing any muscular movement, however small, to spoil or alter the quality of the tone. This it is, which demands so much practice.

The pianist who has studied on the best principles—say, for example, the Tobias Matthay system, knows very well how exceedingly difficult it is to keep the muscles of the hand and arm

[1] Or vibrating breath, which is the same thing.

under complete control. How intensely difficult it is to the begin-
ner, and frequently even to the more advanced student, to play
just one note with one finger, and allow the other four fingers to
remain *quite* passively resting on the keys, and how many months
of continuous work have to be devoted to this one feat. If then,
so much thought and care must be given to gain control over a
part of one's body which can be seen, it is certain that it cannot
be less difficult to control a part which is unseen, and can only
be managed by mental concentration.

In the same way as a would-be pianist begins work by making
soft tones, so should the vocalist begin his voice training by
passing the breath very quietly through the head, and so let the
tone gradually strengthen and improve. How to do this can be
easily seen by closing the mouth and humming a sound, and then
continuing the same sound on *ah* with the lips parted.

The principal of one of the London schools of music once
stated at a lecture, that he taught a certain blind girl to sing who
had previously experienced great difficulty in the matter. After
long delay, he at length gained success with his pupil by making
her hum, and this, he stated, brought about a proper ' shock of
the glottis,'[1] and then the pupil began to make progress. Now
surely it is a most remarkable statement to make, that the mere
closing of the mouth, which in producing sound constitutes
' humming,' can have any effect whatever upon the vocal cords.
Let the reader try for himself : Sing *ah* on any convenient note
quite softly, then close the mouth and try and notice if he can
detect the slightest movement or alteration in the region of the
larynx. Then try the reverse way—hum first and afterwards open
the mouth on the same sound and without taking fresh breath,
and it will be found equally impossible to notice any alteration
whatever in the region where sound is usually supposed to
generate.

Beyond that, in the music libel case already alluded to,
Dr. Henry Hulbert was most definite in stating that there is no
connection whatever between the muscles of the mouth and the
intrinsic muscles of the larynx, and several times during the trial
much ridicule was thrown upon the idea that the pushing forward
of the jaw should have any beneficial influence upon the vocal

---

[1] By ' shock of the glottis ' is meant the approximation of the vocal
cords as the air passes upwards between them.

cords which are situated so far below. If, then, it be an accepted fact that the muscles of the face have no connection with the vocal cords, it would certainly seem very difficult to understand how the mere closing of the lips should bring about a proper ' shock of the glottis,' as this singing master stated.

Now please turn again to Figure 1, and see what really does happen when the mouth is closed. The breath coming up the windpipe cannot escape by the first outlet (the mouth), that being closed ; it must, therefore, either come down the nose or else go through the head and produce a sound in doing so. It will be seen that it is quite easy to go through the head, because the breath will only continue its same upward direction.

Of course the breath can, if desired, be driven forward and downward through the nose without being permitted to go higher in its course, in which case there is no sound ; but it is assuredly an equally simple matter for the breath merely to continue its upward course through the sinuses, and so generate tone.

Quite lately I cured a client who was able to speak only in a whisper, by showing her how to direct her breath, and how to use it. She had been attending a London hospital for five months, without gaining any permanent benefit, yet in two interviews of thirty minutes each she was able to speak firmly and distinctly without any trouble. When first I heard her speak, I noticed the escape of the breath forwards through the mouth, so explained to her that sound is made in the head, not in the throat ; then, having made her hum, she was able in less than thirty minutes to speak in quite a natural manner, and she has never experienced difficulty since.[1]

Another argument which must be dealt with is the medical statement mentioned on page 3, ' that when singing *ah* the nasal passage is hermetically sealed.' Now, mere opinions on such a matter are useless ; they have been given, both for and against, over and over again. After many weeks of thought, I devised a most simple plan for proving once and for all whether the nasal passage is used in singing. Let anyone sing *ah* in a quiet and natural way, and let another person take a laryngoscope or small mirror and hold it close underneath the nostril, and when taken away the mirror will be clouded with the warm breath which has

[1] Further details of this and other cases can be given upon application to me either personally or by letter.

been coming down the passage. It is, therefore, quite clear that the nose is not in any way sealed during the act of singing.

Dr. Holbrook Curtis, in his excellent book, *Voice Building and Tone-Placing*, gives the following interesting conversation between himself and Jean de Reszke : ' On welcoming my dear friend, Jean de Reszke, to my house after his fourth return to our shores, I said to him, " Have your studies during the past year taught you anything which may be of use to me ? " " Yes," he replied, " I find that the great question of the singer's art becomes narrower and narrower all the time, until I can truly say that the great question of singing becomes a question of the nose." ' Our old friend, Geoffrey Chaucer, in the fourteenth century realized this fact,[1] for in the prologue to the Canterbury Tales he writes of the Prioresse in the following words :

> Ful wel sche sang the service divine
> Entuned in hire nose ful semely.'

Let it be emphasized in the mind of the reader that he does not write of a ' nasal twang,' or of her vocal cords or throat, but ' Entuned in her *nose ful semely.*'

It is certain that a perfectly free channel down the nostrils will never produce the so-called ' nasal tone.' This tone is produced by partly closing the nasal passage.

This can frequently be experienced when anyone has a cold in the head. Accumulated mucus stops the free passage of the air, with the result that a so-called ' nasal tone ' is produced. I am aware that it is *possible* to speak clearly with the nose held between the fingers, but such a course if continued for any length of time would certainly have a bad effect upon the muscles around the throat, and singing would quickly come to a full stop under such conditions. Anyone therefore, can try for himself and see that in phonation the breath does come down the nostrils. Of course, a tone with throaty production will not show this so clearly as a quiet note well placed in the middle register.

Another most interesting experiment, and one full of meaning, is the following. Take slowly a full breath, then sing quite quietly any note about the middle of the register. Whilst this note is being sung, suddenly expel the remainder of the breath out of the

---

[1] I am indebted to my friend, Dr. E. J. Bellerby, for drawing my attention to this interesting detail.

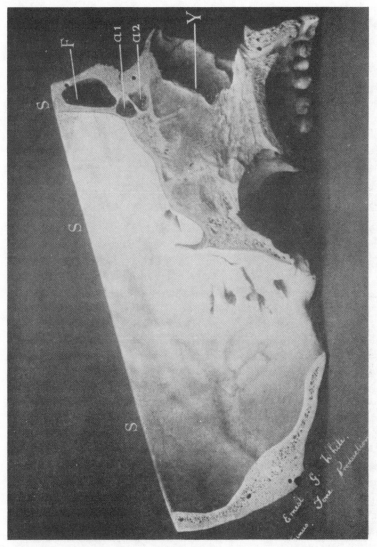

FIGURE 2. LEFT HALF OF SKULL, SHOWING SEPTUM AND FRONTAL SINUS

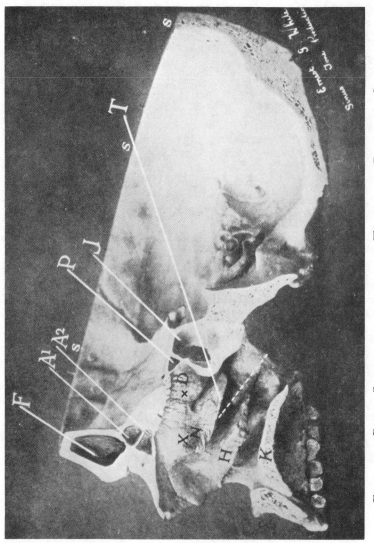

FIGURE 3. RIGHT SIDE OF SKULL, SHOWING TURBINATED BONES AND SINUSES

EXPLANATION OF FIGURES 2, 3 AND 4.

Figures 2 and 3 show the skull cut into halves from back to front. Figure 2 shows the septum, Y, *i.e.*, a thin bony partition which divides the nasal passage down the centre. The corresponding half of the skull (Figure 3) gives a clear view of the structure of the lower part of the cranium. The upper part from the points S has been cut away. It does not affect our work. $A1$, the lower part of the left frontal sinus. $A2$, the upper part of the infundibulum. The corresponding part is seen at $a1$, $a2$, in the left half of the skull. D is the superior turbinated bone, with the superior meatus (or passage) immediately below and behind it.

The posterior ethmoid cells are immediately behind D. P shows part of them. The middle and anterior ethmoid cells take a position in front (*i.e.*, towards the nose) of the posterior, whilst behind is the sphenoid sinus J. N is the middle turbinated bone. The middle meatus is behind and below it.

H is the inferior turbinated bone, and below and behind it is the inferior meatus. The curve of these turbinated bones, and the meatuses which they form, is seen in Figure 4. In this picture we have the skull cut down from ear to ear, that is, at right angles to the cutting shown in Figures 2 and 3. The teeth are clearly seen ; above them is the bone forming the hard palate, whilst immediately above that are the two large curved bones, one on each side, which correspond to H in Figure 3, viz., the inferior turbinated bones. These by their curve form the inferior meatuses. The next pair of bones above are the middle turbinated bones, corresponding to N in Figure 3, and these form the middle meatus on each side. The superior turbinated bones, being very small, cannot be seen in this picture, but it can easily be understood that their position is just above the middle.

The entrance to the maxillary sinus T (Figure 3) is in the middle meatus. This sinus and its formation are also shown in Figures 8 and 9, preceding and facing page 27. Note the depth of the hollow bone (Figure 9) which lies on the book. This bone has been cut away from the skull. In Figure 8 it is shown in a natural state. In Figure 3 the dotted line just below N is referred to in Chapter III, page 73.

C

mouth, and the result will be that immediately the breath comes out through the mouth *only*, the tone will cease. This was the experiment which first gave me the idea that the vocal cords do not produce sound. When I showed this plan to a pupil, he replied, ' Ah ! but of course you *willed* yourself to leave off singing.' I assured him that this was not the case, and then made him work in the same way, and he was bound to acknowledge—as many others have since—that the cessation of sound was not in the least due to volition, but that it was an absolute impossibility under the circumstances to continue it.

What then, is the real explanation of this ? It is simply that when one is singing, the breath is passing through the head and afterwards out at the nose ; but when the breath is directed out of the mouth only, then tone is an utter impossibility.

This can be seen still more plainly in the following manner. Sing the word *shy* on any note of medium pitch. The tone will of course be held on the vowel *i*. Now attempt to sing on the sound *sh* and it will be found quite impossible. The explanation which is usually offered consists in the statement that one cannot vocalize on a consonant. Such a reply cannot be accepted because it is possible to sing on the consonants *l*, *m*, *n* ; and further, the division of sounds into vowels and consonants is merely an arbitrary division of the alphabet which has no bearing upon the subject. In producing the sound *sh* we have the breath coming past the vocal cords and out of the mouth. If the vocal cords produce tone, they ought to produce equally good tone on *sh* as on *i*, for in each case it is quite evident that the breath coming from the lungs is passing the cords. The important point for our consideration is the fact that in *sh* the breath is coming directly out of the mouth, but immediately we cease the *sh* sound and get *i*, the breath alters its course from the mouth, and goes into the head ; that is to say, into the sinuses, and makes its exit through the nose. The word *shy* is not the only one that can be analysed in this way. *Ve*, *se*, *he*, teach the same lesson. While the breath is coming from the mouth for the production of *v*, *s*, or *h*, it is quite impossible to produce tone, but immediately the air escape ceases, tone is produced on *e* or any other vowel that is required. Let it be emphasized that this is not because a vowel is being produced, for if we take the word *no*, tone can be produced on the sound *n* and also on the sound *o*, but in neither case does the

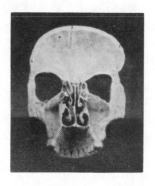

FIGURE 4. TURBINATED BONES, SEPTUM,
AND HARD PALATE

breath come through the mouth. A difficulty which has occurred to several minds is the proved and known fact that when an incision is made in the windpipe below the larynx, tone cannot be produced. ' Here,' said one objector to me, ' is surely a very serious bar to your theories.' Not at all. We know quite well that air will always take its first outlet, and the breath coming up the windpipe will certainly not force itself past the vocal cords when it has an outlet below them.

In this same reasoning we have an explanation of a difficulty which for a very long time I was unable to fathom. If the difference between speech and song be so small, as we have seen on page 12, how can we explain the fact that the one is so easy and the other so difficult ? The answer is that in speech we generally use the sphenoid sinus only. By reference to Figure 18, facing page 37, it will be seen that this is the only sinus which has a completely free and uncovered entrance, and therefore it acts automatically, and without any conscious control on the part of the speaker. The entrances to the ethmoid cells and frontal sinus are placed behind the turbinated bones, and for high notes the air has to travel some distance before it reaches the free and open nasal passage, hence it requires training and skill to bring the air in them into action and under control. When in speaking or singing the breath is not so directed, either consciously or unconsciously, then the result is usually ' clergyman's sore throat,' ' hysterical paralysis of the vocal cords,' or some kindred affection.

The reason of this is not far to seek. Below the tongue is material unsuited for the work of speech and song. Above the tongue is the hard palate of the mouth, the upper surface of which forms the floor of the nasal passage. That passage is divided down the centre by a thin wall known as the septum (see Figures 2 and 4), and each of these passages contains three arched bones known as the upper, middle, and lower turbinated bones. Figure 4 gives a view of these from behind.[1] Then the cheek-bone itself is but the upper surface of a large air chamber having direct communication with the nose. It will be noticed that the whole of this is osseous material, whilst above it are the frontal sinuses over the eyes, the sphenoid sinuses below and behind them, with the ethmoid air cells in front of the sphenoid, but also underneath the

[1] The upper turbinated bones, being very small, can only be seen clearly in Figure 3.

frontal sinuses. Their positions will be seen by referring to Figures
1 and 3. The important and practical point to appreciate is that
the air in all of these is in direct communication with that in the
nose, mouth, and lungs. The whole mass of the structure is bone
of great fineness and beauty, and yet of sufficient.strength.

Now let us think of the material below the tongue, and its
suitability for forming tone. In the first place there is no sinus
anywhere below the tongue where breath could freely vibrate.
There are of course, the two channels, the windpipe and the gullet
(see Figure 1), but each of these has special work to do in passing
food downwards to the stomach, and air to and from the lungs,
and being formed of soft, pliable material, their nature is such that
they are not capable of either producing sound or increasing any
which has been formed.

In *Physiology of the Vocal Registers*, by Golan E. Hoole, we
are told that ' the walls of the resonator are the chest with the
lungs, bronchi, and diaphragm.' Sir St. Clair Thomson, M.D.,
F.R.C.P., in lecturing before the Oxford University Branch of
the Voice Training Society upon ' The Advantages and Necessities of Voice Culture,' in April 1908 also spoke of the chest, the
windpipe, and the larynx, and the pharynx as being resonators.[1]
The lungs, a soft spongy material ; the diaphragm, also a soft,
yielding tissue, and the bronchi, two short tubes leading from the
lungs to the windpipe—how can these increase the tone and so
act as resonators ? The whole of these, including also the larynx
and pharynx, are composed of very soft and sensitive skin and
ligament, and from their very nature are quite incapable of taking
any important part in the increase of tone. Who would take a
tuning fork and, having set it in vibration, put it on a sponge
in order to increase its tone ? What manufacturer would expect
to form a flute or any other sound-producing instrument from
india-rubber ? Yet this is a perfectly legitimate simile to take in
considering either the formation of tone or its increase by any
part of our anatomy below the tongue.

Yet a third person could be cited who speaks of the lips as being
resonators. This is surely equally impossible.

Another point, too, which has been missed by a great many
writers upon this much-discussed matter is : that the breath

[1] He also included—and of course correctly—' the mouth, the nose,
and its accessory cavities in the head.'

contained in the lungs and bronchi is not in a state of vibration, that is to say, it has not yet reached the point when it is turned into tone, for everyone agrees that tone cannot be produced *below* the vocal cords. How, then, can the lungs, diaphragm and bronchi act as resonators to air which has not yet taken any part in producing tone ?

Dr. Henry Hulbert, in lecturing upon ' The Scientific Basis of Voice Culture,' before the Incorporated Society of Musicians in London, on 31st December 1908, said : ' The cords, by vibrating, make the air vibrate (that which passes into the upper air passages, and that which is still in the lower part). This column of vibrating air stretching from the *floor*[1] of the chest to the upper end of the air passage constitutes voice.' He owned that some people would not admit that the breath vibrated below the vocal cords, but he personally was convinced that they were wrong in their objection. As a proof he gave the illustration that when a stone is thrown into a pond, the ripples in the water extend in every direction. Clearly that is correct, but throwing a stone into a pond will not stand as a simile in voice production. In the case of the stone, there is a *displacement* of material caused by the stone entering and sinking in the water, the heavier material displacing the lighter—hence the circles of ripples. In the case of voice production there is no such displacement ; it is merely the moving upwards of a column of air : a movement from the lungs towards the point where it *shall be* set in vibration. One may grant that there may be a very tiny amount of sympathetic vibration in the air column as it comes along the lowest part of the windpipe, but at that particular stage of its journey it is no more engaged in the active work of tonal production than is the drop of water in a mill stream helping to turn the wheel when it is as yet a mile from the mill. The truth is that the idea of vocal cord vibrations, with all its attendant theories, has for generations been accepted as a truism, and men have not taken the trouble to stop and consider whether the path laid out for them by previous masters is right or wrong.

Masters with a keen power of perception between good and bad vocal tone abound. There are hundreds of tutors who fully understand how the best points in a vocal composition should be brought out so as to secure an artistic interpretation, but unless

[1] The italics are mine.

the student possesses the very rare gift of a naturally correct
and free tone-production, much difficulty would probably be
experienced in finding the professor, male or female, who could
put the finger on the exact physical cause of any defect in tone ;
for let it be remembered that if the tone be not good, there is
a physical cause at the root of the matter, and this must be
cleared away before the student can become the artist.

It is therefore a matter of the utmost importance for the would-
be singer to realize that the first step in his vocal equipment should
be an intimate knowledge of the sound-producing machine which
he possesses, and then he may proceed to make himself master of
and to control its every detail : first the skill of the scientific
mechanic, then the glorious artist, beautiful and free.

In the article on singing by M. A. R. Tuker, already quoted, she
states : ' Our would-be singers come out from the academies
with their voices half or wholly ruined ; the deterioration can be
traced while the lessons are in progress.' This is a serious statement to make, but it must be conceded that such is the experience
of a vast number of candidates for musical honours. Nor can this
be wondered at if voice training generally be carried on upon lines
which are opposed to scientific facts and laws.

That the scheme of vocal cord vibrations is in direct opposition to acoustic and physical laws, we hope to show presently.
Mr. Wallworth says, in his book on singing (Hammond & Co.) :
' Voice practice is to develop the muscles and strengthen and make
flexible the larynx generally.' This may be taken as the usual idea
of the object of practising, but it does not coincide with mine.
I should say that voice practice is to ensure a free passage of air
through the vocal sinuses, so that no muscular movement may
mar the tones thus produced.

Again, quoting M. A. R. Tuker's article, it is stated : ' The metal
of a trumpet remains immobile, but the throat is only rendered immobile by an exercise of volition. There is nothing so apparently
unimportant, no movement so slight, that it may not disturb our
instrument.' And how easily that instrument is disturbed ! What
a microscopic trifle will cause a muscle somewhere to disturb the
even passage of the air ! To give any pupil the idea that voice
practice is to ' develop muscles ' is in my opinion one of the worst
of blunders.

Learning to sing is mental, not physical work, although such a plan is in direct opposition to the opinion expressed by Madame Albani. ' Learning to sing is a *real physical strain*[1] ; at any rate until the breathing exercises are mastered,' said that lady to a Press representative just before her farewell concert at the Albert Hall in 1912. As, however, the sole object of the vocalist is the control and direction of a very small column of air, it is evident this cannot require physical energy. In fact, it is physical, *i.e.*, muscular work, which is at the root of all bad tone. If we knew exactly how and where to direct our breath movement, that in itself, and that alone, would produce the best tone which each individual is capable of making.

The pianist does not, perhaps we ought to say, should not, work with the idea of developing and strengthening the muscles of his hand, but rather his object is to get absolute independence of fingers, to be able to control either swift or slow digital movements with an unerring certainty that they will perform his will. Mr. Tobias Matthay, in his excellent work, *The Act of Touch*, says : ' We may rest perfectly assured when we see a performer labouring at his instrument as if he were lifting oxen, that he has certainly not conquered the mere " elements " of using the keyboard correctly, has not learned his technical A B C, however admirable his artistic instincts may be in other ways.' So with the would-be vocalist. His work as a student is to be able to send his breath along with greater or less speed, or to create movement here or there as the knowledge which he should possess directs him. But in all cases this should be done with perfect ease and smoothness, as the result of mechanical control, which goes much further than ' his technical A B C.'

Now let us see what happens when the vocalist attempts to produce a crescendo, not having a full mental perception of the means whereby the louder tone is to be produced. The note having been started, the singer tries to increase the tone, and believing that the vocal cords are the seat of sound, naturally puts a pressure upon the larynx and the windpipe, with the result that both are considerably tightened and constricted, and one frequently may see the whole face and neck of the artist (!) get crimson with the endeavour to produce a big tone. I personally, have seen a strong man come off the platform wiping the dripping perspiration from his forehead in consequence of the huge physical (not

---

[1] The italics are mine.

mental) efforts that he has made during the interpretation of his ballad. Let me quote the *Nineteenth Century and After* for May 1903 :

When the British public sees a favourite ' star ' getting a spasmodic grip of a handy piece of furniture in order to produce her high note *di bravura*, its honest soul is moved at the supreme effort being made for its delectation. For the effort counts as part of the effect. It is listening to a ' star,' so, of course, this is real singing ; but the criterion is as primitive as that of the rustic admirers who shouted to their *primo uomo*, ' Hold it on, Steen,' lest the note being bawled from his throat at the risk of an apoplexy should not last long enough to shame his rival in the village choir. When we sing with effort we may be quite sure we are singing badly. The divine in all art is like the ' still small voice' ' ; the rushing and the tearing and the noise are not yet art. Not until the complex elements given us by the material have been reduced to a simple formula—a simple formula used by a master—is real art achieved ; and when we look or when we hear, we say, ' How simple,' and, if we know, we say, ' How difficult '.

The reason for this unedifying display can be traced in the following simple experiment. Let the reader hold the hand in the position shown in Figure 5, so that the thumb and first finger form, roughly speaking, a circle. Within that circle from *A* to *B* is a column of air. Now let the two fingers press together ; this will produce a tightening and drawing of the muscles of the fingers, but will certainly not have any effect upon the column of air which is enclosed. So it is with singing. The windpipe encloses a column of air, which, when set in vibration by passing around the sinuses, creates tone, but no amount of pressure upon either the larynx or the windpipe will make the air column move with greater speed, which is one of the physical causes of an ascending musical passage, or set a larger column of air in motion, which is the physical cause of a heavier or louder tone. Here we at once have an explanation why vocalists with big voices usually have large throats, viz., because there is a possibility of setting a large column of air in motion, and the function of the vocal cords is to control that column of air and allow a larger or smaller amount to pass upwards as may be required, but they are themselves quite incapable of setting up those tonal vibrations which we term ' voice.'

Provided the student is willing to spend some little time upon the matter, each individual can submit the assertion with respect to the control of air to a personal test. Let him be seated before

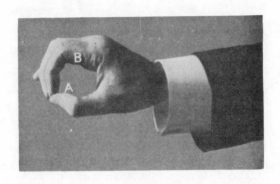

FIGURE 5. AN EXPERIMENT WITH AIR

a skilful operator with the laryngoscope ; then, with the instrument well placed in his mouth, let him sing quietly a single note and then make a crescendo, and it will be found that as the vocal cords separate so the tone increases, thus allowing a larger column of air to pass between them. I am aware that it has been stated by excellent singers that one cannot get a musical singing note while the laryngoscope is in the mouth. Doubtless it is a difficult matter to accomplish, but I know by experience that if sufficient time be devoted to the endeavour, it is possible to produce a proper vocal tone with the mirror in position ; but practice is as necessary for the person on whom the mirror is used as it is for the operator who is using it. Neither can do his work well without frequent attempts and failures.

We have now another serious matter to consider, viz., how, with these theories, can we account for the ' breaks ' in voices and consequent ' registers ' ? It has been stated that registers do not exist by nature, and that ' a break in the voice is an attempt of Nature to assert her forsaken laws against the distortion of them by ignorance and false training.' I doubt whether such a definition would be any assistance to a vocalist who is trying to get rid of his ' breaks.' One flaw in the statement is, that children who have been guiltless of any kind of training whatever, either true or false, frequently exhibit marked breaks. There can be no doubt that with the untrained voice there are breaks or divisions, which are frequently very difficult to smooth away.

I must confess that the consideration of this matter gave me much trouble, but like many other things, the problem when solved seems remarkably easy. Still this only again bears out the truth of the remarks made by Sir William Preece, and alluded to on page 5. Let the reader refer to Figures 1 and 3 facing pages 11 and 17, and he will see the right side sphenoid sinus marked *J*. The passage of the breath around the interior of this cavity creates tone and answers to the lowest register, usually known as the ' chest ' voice. Close by the sphenoid sinuses are some air cells known as the posterior ethmoid cells or sinuses. The entrance to these is situated in the superior meatus, that is a passage in the nose immediately below and behind the superior turbinated bone *D*. Here, then, we have the material for forming the middle notes of the voice.

There is now only the ' head ' voice, or highest register, to consider. In close proximity to the posterior ethmoid cells, in fact divided from them by only a thin transverse bony partition, are two other sets of cells more numerous than the former—these are the middle and anterior ethmoid cells. The entrance to them is in the middle meatus, a passage immediately below the superior, and separated from it by the middle turbinated bone N. These cells are in direct communication with the frontal sinuses F, with which they are connected by means of a long funnel-shaped cellular canal known as the infundibulum. The lower entrance to this canal is, as before stated, in the middle meatus, the exact position being behind the letter N, a little to the left and above it, marked X. Here is the position for the ' head,' or highest register of the voice. By reference to Figure 1, it can now be seen that there is a continuous column of air from the lungs, through the bronchi and trachea, past the larynx, up past the pharynx, into the nose, through the infundibulum, into the forehead just above the eyes. In these three positions, marked in Figures 1 and 3, $J. P, F$, we have all the material that is required for forming vocal tone. In this explanation of ' head ' notes, we can well see the force and correctness of the directions sometimes given by singing masters to ' get the high notes more forward.' As a matter of absolute fact, they are produced in a more forward position, for it is clear, by reference to Figure 3, that the frontal sinuses (where the high notes are produced) are in front of the sphenoid sinuses. The reader should now make a careful study and comparison of Figures 1, 2, 3, and 6. No. 1 shows the head, throat, and lungs, and their relative positions to each other. No. 2 shows the left side of the skull with the septum of the nose in position. No. 3 shows the right side of the skull. The septum not being in position, we see the sphenoid sinus, a very small portion of the posterior ethmoid cells, and the inferior, the middle, and the superior turbinated bones. In Nos. 6 and 7 the superior and middle turbinated bones have been removed, so that we may see the position of the anterior ethmoid cells, the posterior ethmoid cells, and the infundibulum. The arrows show the ostia, or in less technical language, the openings of communication into the nose. It must not be supposed that the figures here given are constant and represent every head. It would probably be correct to say that the unlimited variations which we find in the human face are quite equalled by the varying

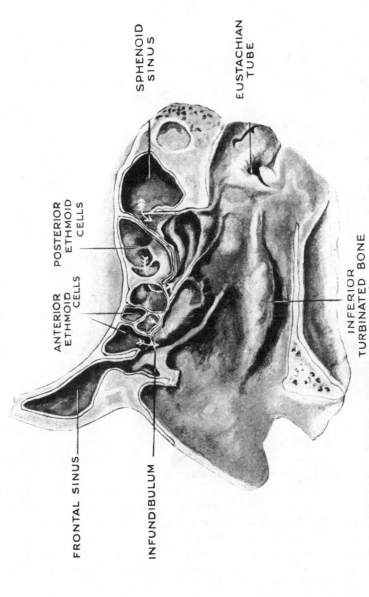

SPHENOID SINUS

EUSTACHIAN TUBE

POSTERIOR ETHMOID CELLS

ANTERIOR ETHMOID CELLS

FRONTAL SINUS

INFUNDIBULUM

INFERIOR TURBINATED BONE

Figure 6. Right Side of Head, With Superior and Middle Turbinated Bones cut away, showing Ethmoid Cells and Infundibulum

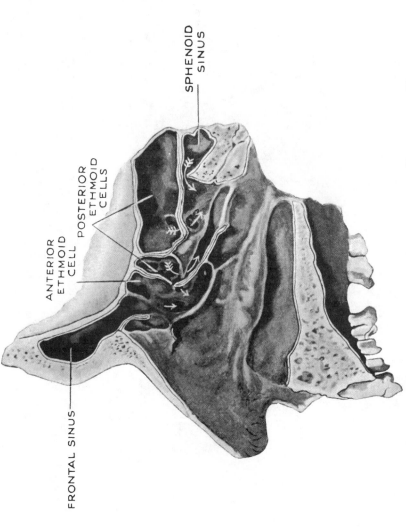

FIGURE 7. RIGHT SIDE OF HEAD, WITH SUPERIOR AND MIDDLE TURBINATED BONES CUT AWAY, SHOWING ETHMOID CELLS AND INFUNDIBULUM

FRONTAL SINUS

ANTERIOR ETHMOID CELL

POSTERIOR ETHMOID CELLS

SPHENOID SINUS

FIGURE 8. SKULL SHOWING MAXILLARY SINUS IN POSITION

FIGURE 9. SKULL SHOWING MAXILLARY SINUS CUT AWAY

dispositions of the sinuses and their surroundings.[1] Figures 6 and 7 show two posterior ethmoid cells ; sometimes there is one only of a fairly large size, or there may be three. In the anterior groups there may be as many as seven, eight, or even nine cells, and these usually have several communications into the nose.

It is a matter of more than passing interest to notice how all these anatomical details entirely coincide with the statement made by Dr. Holbrook Curtis that ' no voice can be injured by carrying the head quality too low.'

The maxillary sinus or antrum of Highmore (Figure 3, *T*) is of immense importance in increasing the tone, that is to say, in acting as a resonator. The sinus itself is formed within the maxillary bone, familiarly known as the ' cheek-bone ' ; the entrance to it from the middle meatus of the nose is very small,[2] but the cavity itself is of considerable size. Both the size of the cavity and its exact position can be seen by referring to Figures 3, 8, and 9. In No. 3 the entrance to the cavity from the mouth is shown at *T*. In life the entrance is not as large as it appears to be in the photograph, because it is partly closed by membrane. In No. 8 the maxillary bone is seen in its natural position and in No. 9 it is cut off in order to show the depth and size of the sinus. The piece which has been cut off rests upon the book, whilst the entrance to the chamber can be seen in the skull itself.

This sinus is developed very early in life. At the time of teething the cavity is so small that it would hardly accommodate an orange pip, but at the period of the second dentition the antrum assumes its full growth, and reaches its complete or adult form about the age of 25 years. It is an interesting and significant fact that at birth the maxillary sinus is the most complete part of the vocal apparatus—looking, of course, upon the head, not the larynx, as the seat of sound. In the first days of our existence the ethmoid cells are present, but in an elementary stage of development, whilst the frontal and sphenoid sinuses, as such, are absolutely non-existent, although the material for forming them is present. The ethmoid cells form first, that is to say, the material for the middle register of the voice, then the frontal sinuses begin to develop as extensions of the anterior ethmoid cells, and at about

[1] Appendix A, page 163.
[2] Had the entrance been a large one, the usefulness of the cavity as a resonator would have been lessened.

28   SCIENCE AND SINGING

the sixth or seventh year they may be recognized as distinct cavities. Lastly come the sphenoid sinuses at about the age of 14. The frontal sinuses reach their full development at about the twentieth year. Thus the musical machinery gradually increases, and so of course does the power to sing. Here then, with this simple idea of creating air movement in these different sinuses, we have the ' complex elements given us by the material, reduced to a simple formula,' and those who work on these lines will find that by these means indeed ' is real art achieved.' The vocal results to be obtained by work and practice on these lines are nothing less than astonishing.

Let the student, however—and the master—beware of expecting an easy and comfortable path to tread because the formula is simple. Indeed, we would say with Mr. Pickwick, that the work ' comprises in itself a difficult study of no inconsiderable magnitude.' Problems for solution will turn up at point after point in almost endless variety, but, providing he knows how, the difficulties can be overcome by the student with patience and perseverance, and the voice will be found to improve both in tone and strength, while the act of singing becomes more and more easy. Providing he knows how !

' Aye, there's the rub ! ' Then, let me give some rules for the guidance of those who really seek the truth. I say, seek the truth, advisedly, because it will not be found on the surface ; for ' Nature has buried truth deep in the bottom of the sea.' Therefore, the searcher must not expect to find the voice fully developed by these means in a week or a month, for continuous application is necessary ; but this method has never caused anyone to say, as I have known vocalists say, ' I never practise now, for I find that the more I practise the worse I become,' or again, ' My voice was better before I had lessons than it was after.'

Firstly then, let the reader remember the difference in the size of the entrance to the sphenoid sinus and the entrance to the ethmoid cells. The latter are much smaller.[1] This brings us to the consideration of acoustic laws, and it will be seen how beautifully and exquisitely an all-wise Creator has arranged these matters to coincide and harmonize. My scientific readers will understand

[1] This cannot very well be shown by a picture ; an examination of a real skull is necessary.

FIGURE 10. SOUND FIGURES

what I mean when I say that the higher in pitch a sound is, so much the smaller is the shape of that sound.

One is probably correct in saying that comparatively few people realize that sound has a definite and distinct shape. We know that our coat and our shoes have shape, for we can see and feel them, but the fact that sound has a shape is not so obvious. A pretty and interesting method of giving sound a visible shape is that known as Chladni's figures. In this experiment a glass or a metal plate is suitably clamped to a table. It is then lightly covered with fine sand. If a violin bow be drawn along the edge of the plate it produces a musical sound, and the vibrations of the plate make the sand collect into ridges forming patterns on the plate as shown in Figure 10. The varying patterns are produced by different notes. The beautiful balance of the figures surely shows the exquisite symmetry of nature's working.

Another experiment which shows the shape of sound, and which is more useful to our purpose, is that known as the manometric flames. The material for the experiment consists of four mirrors about six inches square arranged as a box (see Figure 11), which is fixed on a revolving table, and by means of gearing is made to rotate by turning a small handle.

Also a round metal box about two inches in diameter and three-eighths of an inch in thickness is required. This is divided into halves by a piece of thin silk of the same diameter as the box. To one side of the box two small metal tubes are fixed (E and G), one of which (G, at the edge of the box) serves as an inlet for gas, and the other (E, in the centre of the box, and on the same side of it as G) ends in an ordinary gas burner. To the other side of the box is attached some india-rubber piping, to which is affixed a mouthpiece H. For use, the gas burner is placed on a level with the mirrors by sliding it into position on the rod F F and fixing it with a small screw. Then, having lit the gas, place the receiver H to the mouth and sing any moderately low note to the vowel sound *ah*, at the same time rotating the mirrors, which should be placed immediately in front of the gas jet. The flame will then appear as at A in Figure 12.

Now alter the note to the octave above, still rotating the mirror, and the flame will change to the shape shown at B. Here we have a practical demonstration of a most important law which should be known to every singer, viz., that in an ascending passage the

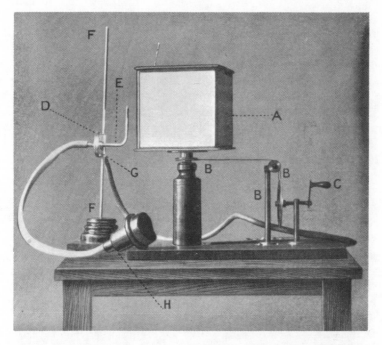

FIGURE 11. MATERIAL FOR SHOWING MANOMETRIC FLAMES

A. Revolving box, having a mirror for each of its four sides.
B, B, B. Gearing, by means of which the handle C rotates the mirrors.
D. Metal box, divided into halves by a piece of silk of the same diameter as the box.
E. Metal tube fixed into the box, and ending in a gas burner.
F. Metal rod fixed into a heavy wooden base. The box D can slide up or down on the rod F, F, and be fixed at any point by a small screw.
G. Small metal tube for gas inlet (to which piping is attached) inserted into box D on the same side of the division as tube E.
H. Mouthpiece connected with piping, the metal tube for which is fixed on the opposite side of box D.

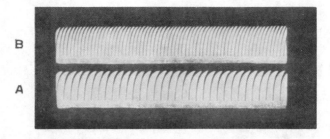

FIGURE 12. PHOTOGRAPH OF MANOMETRIC FLAMES

shape of the sound must be made smaller. In this little experiment we have the singing breath on one side of the box, playing through the silk upon the gas which is the other side of the box. The result is a flame of which Figure 12 is a photograph.

The question might be asked : ' But can I do this ? ' Yes, certainly ; you cannot go from one note to its octave without doing it, either consciously or unconsciously. You must do it, in order to produce the sound at all—it is one of Nature's laws that you shall do it, but if you *know* that you have to do it, and realize it, then you endeavour to work with Nature, and you are not, either consciously or unconsciously, working against her. Thus what before was hard work, in consequence of the strain put upon your muscular and physical self, now becomes easy because you are knowingly working on scientific and natural laws.

Now it follows that if the column of air be smaller, it must therefore, take less pressure or exertion to move it. Therefore be careful that there must be less breath or wind pressure—so to speak—for a high note than for a low note. This is, of course, at variance with a great deal of present-day teaching. People frequently think that the higher the note required, the greater the exertion necessary for the production of that note, and the greater the amount of breath that must be used. When a top note is wanted, the advice often given is, ' Take a big breath and go for it.' Are such principles artistic, or in accordance with even elementary laws of acoustics ? Which pipe in a church organ will produce a high note, the long, big pipe, or the little, baby pipe ? Most people know that the big pipes produce the low notes and require the most wind. Anyone who doubts this statement might attempt to blow the bellows of a church organ, and he will soon be convinced of the reality of the matter.

An interesting scientific fact, bearing upon this matter, is mentioned by Dr. A. Guillemin in his book, *Generation de la Voix et du Timbre*.[1] He tells us that, according to the experiments in acoustics made by Ch. Lootens, there are two methods of raising the pitch of a note. One is by making the air travel at a greater rate. This, of course, implies increased breath-pressure, and consequent danger of physical strain. The second method is by the breath travelling in smaller curves. This implies a lessening

[1] Félix Alcan, Paris.

of breath-pressure, and a consequent ease of production and purity of tone.

Now let us direct our attention to the head register. The explanation of this is that the air column is made to travel chiefly via the frontal sinus, and the course which leads directly to it, leaving the other passages comparatively speaking unused. Not that any part of the instrument is at any time idle during tone production; it is merely a case of to what extent each sinus is used. For the *lowest* register or series of notes, the sphenoid sinuses marked J (Figures 1 and 3) are the chief factors, whilst the ethmoid air cells and the frontal sinuses, marked respectively P and $F F$, play a less important part. For the middle register, the posterior ethmoid cells are chiefly responsible, while the other parts are less used; and again for the highest register the frontal sinuses with the middle and anterior ethmoid cells are the chief medium for tone, while the remainder do merely a small though important share in the work. Now when the breath suddenly leaves one position and takes up another, then we have what is known as, and actually is, ' a break.' When the breath can pass easily, freely, and gradually from one position to another, without making any sudden change in the placing, then we get the smooth, even voice of one quality throughout its compass, which is so difficult to attain.

Here then, we have a threefold cord, and Solomon tells us that such ' is not quickly broken.' There are the three positions working not separately but together, and in harmony with each other, each one forming its stream of vibrating air, the three streams eventually uniting to form one column of tone, and unless the master and the student are capable of knowing and hearing that the right proportion of work is done by each part, bad or poor tone is sure to be the result.

That well-known and much respected teacher, the late Mr. Charles Lunn, makes some excellent remarks upon the subject of registers in his book *Philosophy of Voice*. He says: ' Just as a pianist knows which hand he will use, and never confuses between one hand and the other, so is a vocalist with his registers; and just as a listener cannot tell by sound which hand is in use, so a listener should not be able to tell by sound which register is in use.' Perhaps an even better simile than the foregoing is that of a violinist, who, with his four strings, produces an even range of notes from the highest to the lowest. The length of string varies as he moves from one position to another, but the quality of the tone remains unaltered. So with the vocalist : he plays with his column of breath into one sinus or another and varies the air pressure according to which sinus he is using. The student of course has to learn consciously to make these differences with respect to the position of the air column, also its pressure and its shape. The artist, having complete control over his instrument, makes the necessary physical alterations coincide with his musical requirements, but does so unconsciously, in the same way that an educated person uses correct grammar unconsciously.

It has been frequently stated that we do not possess any *conscious* control over these three positions. The reply to this criticism is very simple ; for, if, for the sake of argument, we consider the statement to be correct, we are, even so, in a position no worse than is the person who works upon vocal cord theories.

For centuries we have been trying to get control over the vocal cords, but we have certainly not succeeded up to the present. In a book named *The Voice*, written by W. A. Aikin (M.D. Brux., L.R.C.P. London, M.R.C.S.), we read as follows : ' The vocal cords are not directly under the guidance of the will. We play upon them by ear, and we have no other means of controlling them than through the sense of hearing.'

Thus it must be acknowledged that the criticism as to want of control over the sinus-positions is, to say the least, a very poor one. It is however, worse than poor ; it is incorrect. The skilled craftsman, who is an adept at his particular work, can do things and produce results which the uninitiated might deem impossible ; and those who have studied the art of Sinus Tone Production have as much command over these positions as a skilled pianist has over his fingers. Over and over again have I been asked: 'But *how* do you control the positions ? ' It is difficult to supply an enquiring mind with an exact solution of the problem, but it can be met, as many a question has been met, by asking another : ' How is it that a blade of grass springs from a speck of seed ? ' No logical reply can be given, but we know by experience that grass does so grow. Professor C. A. Young, writing of mysteries in Nature, says :

Do not understand me at all as saying that there is no mystery about the planets' motions. There is just the one single mystery—gravitation,

D

and it is a very profound one. How it is that an atom of matter can attract another atom, no matter how great the distance, no matter what intervening substance there may be, how it will act upon it, or, at least, behave as if it acted upon it, I do not know, I cannot tell. Whether they are pushed together by means of an intervening ether, or what is the action, I cannot understand. It stands with me along with the fact that when I will that my arm shall rise, it rises. It is inscrutable. All the explanations that have been given of it seem to me merely to darken counsel with words and no understanding. They do not remove the difficulty at all. If I were to say what I really believe, it would be that the motions of the spheres of the material universe stand in some such relation to Him in Whom all things exist, the ever present and omnipotent God, as the motions of my body do to my will ; I do not know how, and never expect to know.

From the same standpoint one may admit it is difficult to explain in so many words exactly *how* the sinuses are controlled, although in a later chapter the matter is put upon an intelligible basis, and, we think, with considerable success.

For the present, however, we will be content with pointing out that the theory makes, at all events, no serious demands upon our credulity, for we know that even a child is able, without any training, to direct the breath either out of the mouth or down the nose at will without making any conscious physical movement. That much we are bound to admit. If then will power is able to change the position of our breath movement from the mouth to the nose, surely the same power can move a step higher, viz., from the nose to the sinus. The proposition is absolutely reasonable, and practice endorses the theory.

As might be expected, the sinuses and cells show in different people an infinite variety both in size and shape ; this accounts for the different shades of tone and timbre which make individuality. It is interesting to note, that with the aboriginal Australians and the Maoris the frontal sinuses are seldom developed. Writing on this matter Dr. Logan Turner says : ' It has been suggested that the somewhat flat character of the voice in these native tribes is due to the absence or feeble development of the nasal air sinuses.' Undoubtedly the suggestion is correct and harmonizes well with the theories of Sinus Tone Production.

Figures 6, 7, and 13 show what immense variety of shape is found in different frontal sinuses. The originals of Figure 13 are to be found in the Museum of the Royal College of Surgeons. Permission was kindly accorded the author to reproduce these in

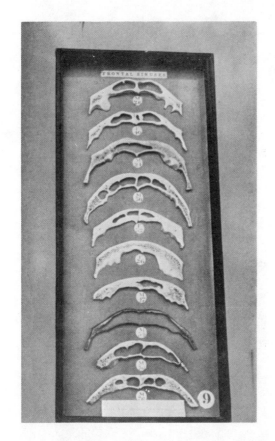

FIGURE 13. FRONTAL SINUSES

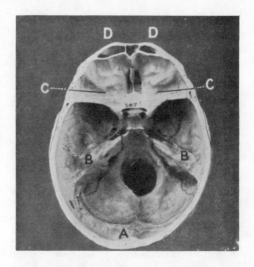

FIGURE 14. SKULL SHOWING SIZE AND SHAPE OF FRONTAL
SINUS FROM ABOVE

FIGURE 15. COMPLETE SKULL

this work, and also Figures 4 and 14. Figure 13 shows slices cut off the front part of the skull of men and women. Each one is labelled *M* or *F*, with the respective age of each person. The sixth specimen (counting downwards) gives us an example of a skull not having any frontal sinus. Such a condition is met only rarely in civilized peoples. The manner in which the ten specimens have been sliced off will be clear by reference to Figure 14. In this the whole top of the skull has been cut off. *A* is the back part of the head. *B B* is the auditory mechanism. The whole space from *C C* forwards to *D D* comprises the frontal sinuses, and it will be seen what a large amount of space they occupy. Their depth can be seen in Figures 2 and 3. Figures 15, 16, and 17 will probably give further assistance in making the position and size of these sinuses clear. No. 15 shows the skull complete, but the place over the right eye where it has been cut is easily noticed. Nos. 16 and 17 show the bone cut away and the sinuses left visible. The varying sizes of these sinuses will easily account also for the fact of tenor, bass, and baritone voices. The tenor vocalist will probably have large frontal sinuses but small sphenoid, while the reverse will be the case with the bass singer. The baritone will have a fairly equal development. One cannot of course, actually prove the truth of these hypotheses, except by postmortem examinations on capable singers. Whether any will be found sufficiently imbued with the spirit of scientific research and development as to make arrangements for their cranium to go into the hands of the anatomist at their decease, is perhaps slightly doubtful. Be that as it may, the theories certainly seem to be sound, and in accord with anatomical facts. Compare carefully Figures 6 and 7. In the former there is but a very narrow passage into the frontal sinus in consequence of the prominence of the nasal crest. In Figure 7 there is no such crest, consequently there is a wide opening into the sinus. Under such conditions a tenor voice would be impossible. An opening so wide would prevent the shaping of a tenor sound (see manometric flames, facing page 30). In Figure 7 it is very improbable that the sinus conditions would produce even a good baritone voice. The sphenoid sinus is small and underneath a posterior ethmoid cell, whilst the anterior ethmoid cells seem to be poorly developed. The musical possibilities of this skull would certainly be far inferior to those of Figure 6.

A point that is worthy of much consideration in studying this part of our subject, is the fact that in a child's head there is no sphenoid sinus. The four bones which form the two cells (one cell on each side) exist only separately until puberty. Here at once is the physical reason for boys' voices being soprano, because they use chiefly the frontal sinuses. Their low notes are invariably weak, because they lack the physical means for making them strong. When, at the age of fourteen or fifteen, the new sinuses begin to form and come into use, one can quite understand the difficulty that the air column would then have in accommodating itself to the new conditions, because there will now be three positions for it to use, instead of two as heretofore.

A similar train of thought can be used with respect to girls. It would be unwise to go so far as to say that there has never been a young girl contralto, but such a voice is very seldom heard. One may frequently meet with girls whose voices have had the lower register forced down—probably and invariably to accommodate school songs where B, B flat, or even A is sometimes written, but a genuine girl contralto is indeed a *rara avis*. The reason is the same as that given for boys' voices ; viz., that the material for producing the lowest notes has not yet been formed. I do not mean by this that it is impossible to sing a low note without the sphenoid sinuses. A well-trained singer can produce one-and-a-half or two octaves of tone simply with the frontal sinuses, but in this case the tone would be very thin and ineffective in the lowest register. This explanation of the so-called ' breaking ' of the voice at the age of puberty seems to the writer a much more reasonable idea than the usually accepted theory that the vocal cords themselves break. At this age both the muscular and bony parts of the body are undergoing rapid and pronounced development. Not only do the sphenoid sinuses form, but the other sinuses get considerably larger, whilst the whole body increases both in size and strength. How very improbable, then, it seems that whilst our body as a whole is undoubtedly developing and getting stronger, our vocal cords should ' break ' and get weaker. Moreover, laryngoscopic investigation has failed to detect any sign of ' breaking ' at this age.

There is undoubtedly a marked difference between the vocal cords of a boy of fourteen and a lad of ten, but the difference consists chiefly in the fact that whilst the younger boy has cords

FIGURE 16. SKULL WITH BONE OVER THE RIGHT EYE CUT
AWAY, THUS SHOWING THE FRONTAL SINUS

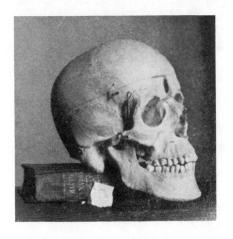

FIGURE 17. THE SAME AS FIGURE 16, BUT IN A DIFFERENT
POSITION

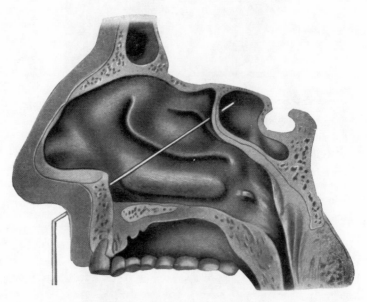

FIGURE 18. PROBE SHOWING ENTRANCE TO SPHENOID SINUS

The probe is placed up the nostril, and is here seen entering the sphenoid sinus. The bone which forms the left wall of the sinus has been taken away, so as to show the shape and size of the cavity and the probe within it.

of the usual white colour, which act quickly in phonation, the older one has cords which are slightly red, and they are slower in action. But the mere fact that they are in the process of lengthening is quite sufficient to account for these points.

The same line of thought will give a reasonable and satisfying explanation for the soprano voices of the old *castrati*. It has always seemed very remarkable that an operation performed so far away from the seat of sound should have so much effect upon the vocal cords. But, looking upon the matter from the standpoint of head production, we see that such an operation would naturally have the effect of preventing a full bodily development over the whole physical system; which means that the bones which form the sphenoid sinuses would not come together, consequently the sound box for forming the low notes would be absent. In all probability, the other sinuses also would not come to a full size, although they would doubtless increase. The question however, is not an important matter from a practical point of view. I firmly believe the idea is correct, but should it eventually prove otherwise, the main burden of this book, that sound is produced by air vibration in the head, will still hold good and true.

We now come to a very interesting stage in the unfolding of our plans. It has been said that singing masters each consider their own particular ' method ' as the only possibly correct one, and consequently all others are wrong. It is therefore very pleasurable to be able to endorse many notes from the late Mr. Charles Lunn's book already quoted. It was never my good fortune to have lessons from him, but I have heard that he did much good work. In my opinion, one of the chief reasons for Mr. Lunn's success was the fact that he insisted strongly upon *downward* thought. He says : ' Think *down* to meet the tone, the body will do the upward pressure.' Again : ' First *think*. Take mental aim from above,' and in another part of the book : ' Our minds have to act downwards to *undo* the natural resistance.' In reply to a question, ' What is the first step after poising the parts ? ' the answer is : ' The first step is thinking downwards as contrasted with the upward thought in an aspirate and other consonants. It is reversing the direction of vital force.' Here we have a rule insisted upon, which is of the utmost importance for the development of good tone. Now place this rule of downward thought side by side with the theory of head production and see how exactly the two agree.

If the column of air be pushed upward from below, there is sure to be a resistance set up at some point in its passage. A kink in the column will be formed somewhere, because the way through is so tortuous. It is in fact because the way is tortuous that the air is set in vibration. An example of this pressure can be seen with a solitaire board, which usually has a groove around its edge, in which marbles can be placed. Let the reader place, say, half a dozen marbles in this groove, and then take the hindmost and endeavour to push the other five forward with it, and it will be found that one of the marbles will probably be pushed off the board. For a similar reason, a locomotive rarely pushes the carriages in front of it, but starts in front and draws them after, when, of course, they can be moved with ease and safety. Perhaps the readiest way of seeing the idea is to take a piece of string or cotton about one or two feet in length, place it on the table and endeavour to push it along from behind. The only effect will be that it will go into a variety of curves or angles. But it can at once be *drawn* along without any difficulty, although it cannot be pushed. So I say, when the column of air is pushed upward from below, a resistance is sure to be set up at some point, creating friction with the muscles and a consequent strain, and loss of vocal tone. Now by working the reverse way, and starting the breath downwards from the points $X\ X$, see Figure 3, there is then simply a straight course to run, and as Nature abhors a vacuum, the breath from below is bound to follow on behind that which has already been used, and so there is a continuous flow of tone (that is, of breath around the sinuses) until the lungs want refilling.[1] Figure 18, facing page 37, will clearly show how difficult it would be to set a column of air travelling into the sphenoid sinus by upward pressure from below.

By starting the air column from below, its passage would be upwards, but it would run *past* the sphenoid sinus, thus producing a comparatively small effect upon the air which that cavity already contains. Let the vocalist realize that all he has to do, is to draw forward the air which is in the sinus. By so doing it travels downwards along the line of the probe, and of necessity the air which is behind it comes along and at once fills the space which it had one second before occupied. Thus a continuous flow of breath around the cavity is secured, which in itself constitutes tone.

[1] Appendix B, page 164.

Let the mind of the student be closely fixed on this drawing downward and forward movement, and then he will get at the very root of the matter : that is to say, an intelligent concentration will be focussed upon the cause of sound, instead of a somewhat hazy endeavour somehow or other to produce a certain much-to-be-desired result, without feeling at all clear how he is to set about it. It is a case of cause and effect. The desired effect is good tone, the question is what is the *physical* cause ?

The explanation just given will be found to give a true and satisfactory solution of the problem, viz., that the mind of the student shall be earnestly fixed on simply drawing the breath downwards from the various sinuses. This simple act constitutes singing, and the cause, not the result, must be the one and only matter which occupies the student's mind.[1]

The first sound which is produced on these lines will be a very small one indeed, and the student invariably has very serious doubts as to the possibility of such a tiny tone ever increasing into a big voice. To quiet such fears, let the pupil be shown an acorn, and then ask the doubter if in the tiny thing which is being held in the hand there is any appearance of a huge oak tree, large enough to shelter hundreds of people. Saint Gregory says : ' Who would imagine that from a single grain of seed a huge tree would rise up, unless he had it as a certain fact by experience ? In the extreme minuteness of the grain where is the hardness of the wood buried, the roughness of the bark, the greenness of the root, the savour of the fruit, the sweetness of the scents, the variety of the colours, the softness of the leaves ? Yet, because we know this by experience, we do not doubt that all these spring from a single grain of seed.' So again one might take a hyacinth bulb as an example of Nature's power of development. Who would expect a lovely flower with an exquisite perfume to grow simply because the bulb is put into the ground ? Yet we know by experience that this takes place.

So, with patient work, it will be found that a big voice of splendid, vigorous tone and quality will develop from this first tiny sound. From it come the possibilities of the sympathetic voice and the martial voice, of the tone of tenderness and the declamatory tone. All come from this tiny seed. And so we again face the great fact that ' Nothing is so grand as truth, nothing so

[1] Appendix C, page 164.

forcible, nothing so novel.'[1] Years ago, Schiller said : ' It is only
through the morning gate of the beautiful that you can penetrate
into the realm of knowledge and power. That which we first feel
to be beauty, will one day be known as truth and strength.' Let
this morning gate of the beautiful be constantly in the mind of
the vocal student, for there is no other way of obtaining that
strength and power which is worth the having.

It is rather curious that in most matters we are content to allow
great things to grow gradually from small. A successful business
is built up by slow degrees ; a house is completed one brick at a
time ; an artist in drawing has many years of work in front of him
before he can gain or even claim any position as a painter, but the
would-be vocalist is, frequently, started at full pressure of voice
and power, under the idea that this means development ; and in
a few months, or possibly even weeks, finds himself landed at
oratorio or opera, regardless of the fact that voices like oaks, ' a
length of years demand.' Here again, as in all details, there is a
physical reason for the necessity of slow procedure.

All the sinuses are lined with mucous membrane, and the mucus
which this membrane generates would, in time, fill the cavities
were it not for the passing of air through them, which thus keeps
them more or less clear, as a brush in sweeping a room.

Cases have been known where people, through long solitary
confinement or captivity, have lost or nearly lost the power of
speech. This cannot be in consequence of the vocal cords ceasing
to act, because they are continually on the move with the mere act
of breathing. The reason is to be found in the fact that the person,
never having any cause for speech, or making sounds, has not set in
movement the breath above the nostrils, that being the highest
point the air column can reach without making sound, therefore the
sinuses and air cells get choked. Silence, then, means a cessation
of breath travelling around the voice cavities in the head, consequently the sinuses become filled with mucus, and the passages
whereby breath can create tone are lost. Now the act of speaking
is too intermittent to keep up the steady flow of air which would
keep the passages sufficiently free for singing. So when the vocalist
begins practising on proper lines there is almost sure to be some,
and perhaps a considerable, amount of phlegm come into the
mouth. As time goes on the flow of mucus decreases, whilst the

[1] Landor, *Imaginary Conversations* : Epictetus and Seneca.

amount of tone increases, because the passages have become clearer. Yet it must be remembered that when the boxes or cells are clear, they will want continual attention to keep them clear. A room once swept and dusted does not henceforth remain clean.

An interesting and by no means unimportant point in tone production on these lines is the fact that the membrane with which all these cavities—including the maxillary—are lined, is much thinner and less vascular than the nasal mucous membrane. In fact, it contains hardly any glands at all. Dr. McLellan, in his *Regional Anatomy*, says : ' The lining membrane within the cells and sinuses is very thin and pale, and very different from the proper lining of the nose.' The result gained to vocal tone by this provision of Nature is that the sound is more brilliant and telling. Had the membrane continued throughout of the same thickness and quality as in the nasal lining, then the tone would be small and thin, through having for its creation a softened sinus, whilst had the membrane been thin throughout, as in the sinuses, then the nasal passages would have lost their power of purifying the air as it passes through the nostrils on its way to the lungs.

When the voice is started at full pressure at the commencement of its training, the air column not being able to get through the very tiny space which is free, a reflex pressure is made, with consequent tightening of the muscles as they feel the backward· pressure. A struggling crowd of people trying to get through the narrow exit of a concert hall or theatre offers an excellent illustration of this matter. The lungs are capable of holding a considerable amount of air, so is a concert hall capable of holding a considerable number of people. There is only one exit from each lung, *i.e.*, along the bronchus. The passages of the two bronchi *B B* (Figure 1) converge into one at the windpipe. Most people have heard of the terrible disasters that follow when, through panic or some other cause, two streams of people trying to make a rapid exit from a hall converge into one narrow passage. The outlet gets packed so tightly that there is practically no progress, whilst the pressure of people from behind continues and perhaps gets worse. An accident of some kind is sure to follow. So is it with singing. If any physical effort be made to force the air along from below, then the windpipe and larynx get blocked with the two currents of air which are being driven along. Naturally very little progress is felt ; then still greater efforts are made to force the breath

through its channel, the consequence being that a still greater
block is effected. So the delicate muscles in this region are strained
and placed at such tension that inflammation and other troubles
are generated, and frequently a doctor has to be sought in order
to get the throat into a healthy condition again. He usually, and
quite correctly, orders rest, after which the whole process may
possibly be repeated. But if the column of air be drawn downward from the points $X\ X$ in Figure 3, then the whole of the
column behind and below it follows quietly on, and there is
neither pressure nor struggle at any point, because there is no
pressure upwards from the lungs, the whole machinery thus
acting automatically.

A very practical and interesting fact which bears upon this
matter is mentioned by Mr. Albert Bach in his book, *Musical
Education and Vocal Culture*. He says:

When in Milan in 1877, I became acquainted with a Russian bass
singer, Mr. Bedenka, who had a voice of great—yet a body of still
greater—compass. He was a passionate smoker, and fond of making
his stoutness a plea for indulging in the weed, maintaining as he did,
that persistent smoking would relieve him in some measure of his
bulk—an expectation which, by the way, he did his best to frustrate
by the gigantic appetite he developed, especially after every singing
lesson.

' Look,' he said one day to me, taking a tremendous whiff from his
long Turkish meerschaum, ' look, how I am living on smoke.' (I must
mention here that Russians do not smoke like the Western nations, but
that they completely inhale the smoke into their lungs.)

Thus, having filled his mouth with a large volume of smoke, he spoke
to me a few words in Russian. These I did not understand, but they
gave me the opportunity of observing the most remarkable fact that,
although he was talking, none of the inhaled smoke reappeared from
the mouth. He had accordingly entirely closed his glottis.

The author then proceeds to explain how in his opinion the man
had been able to speak, notwithstanding the fact that he had
previously entirely closed his glottis.

His solution is that the passage from the lungs being completely blocked, the vocalist had created tone ' by the alternating
condensation and rarefaction of the air contained in the cavity
of the mouth '.

But a glance at such a statement shows the impossibility of
accepting it. An ' alternating condensation and rarefaction of the

air ' can only take place when there is an exciting cause to create
the disturbance.

For example, in playing a flute, the free, straight passage of the
column of air which leaves the lips is sent off at a right angle when
it touches the wooden barrel of the instrument. Hence the
musical tone, that is to say, the ' alternating condensation and
rarefaction of the air.' The rapid vibrations of a piano or violin
string produce similar atmospheric conditions.

But it is quite clear that the mouth has no machinery that
could set up such a movement. From a practical point of view,
therefore, it is evident that the explanation given by Mr. Albert
Bach cannot be accepted as satisfactory.

The truth of the matter is really very simple. Mr. Bedenka had
certainly drawn the tobacco smoke into his lungs, and imprisoned
it there by closing the vocal cords.

But, although the air below the larynx was not available, because
the vocal cords had closed the outlet, yet that which was in the
sinuses was free, and by drawing this air downwards from the
cranial cavities as already explained, the singer could, of course,
create sound.

How simple this explanation seems !

Yet the practical work of keeping all the air-passages free from
pressure in singing is not at all easy. Nevertheless, it is only when
an absolutely free and unimpeded movement of the vocal machinery has been attained, that a voice of beauty and full power is
possible.

Let me now again quote from that valuable book, *The Act of
Touch.*   It is stated (page 102) : ' The fact should at once be
thoroughly recognized and mastered . . . . that we cannot exert
muscular force in any direction with full effect unless we provide
a *basis* firm enough to take without flinching the recoil that super-
venes with equal force in the opposite direction.' If the reader
will carefully think the matter over, it will be seen that it must be
very difficult to put any muscular force upon a *moving* column of
air with a completely free outlet. However, in the endeavour
which many people make to exert muscular force in order to
produce tone, the lungs are the only basis upon which the air
column can rest, and these are certainly not ' firm enough to take
without flinching ' a recoil of any sort.

Would anyone have an idea that special muscular development

is required in order to paint a picture ? Surely not ! Yet the weight of the column of air which creates the tone is considerably less than the weight of the brush and paint with which the artist forms the picture. This suggestion has been found very useful in showing the absurdity of making physical effort in singing. It is the mental effort that is necessary in controlling the activity of the breath, as in guiding the brush.

If the student is to gain that absolute control over the breath-column which is so essential for the production of good and pure tone, he must have very definite ideas as to the exact position to which that activity should be directed, otherwise a friction, a tenseness, or a resistance will be set up somewhere, for we may be assured that it is in the highest degree improbable that the activity will automatically find its way to the correct position.

It may be granted that such cases have been known, and many people could be mentioned, who, without training, have possessed a naturally well-placed voice. It is, however, such a person who constitutes the vocal genius, and the very essence of this volume is to show the musical student how he or she—not being a genius—may follow in the same pathway as those more fortunate people who, automatically, and quite unconsciously, invariably use the best and most correct placing for the different notes which constitute their voice.

The remark has frequently been made to me, that ' we ought *naturally* to use our voices correctly without training.' I will not dispute as to what we ought to do ; it is sufficient to know the fact that we cannot be sure of making really good tone unless we have learned to do so. Neither indeed, does the average person do anything really well unless tuition has been received.

That well-known and much respected vocal specialist, the late Dr. W. G. McNaught, has stated that ' listening to good tone helps a student to reproduce it more than volumes of print or the most skilful verbal instruction.' This opinion is doubtless correct, if the vocal cords be looked upon as the seat of sound, but under the system of Sinus Tone Production the student is shown the physical cause of any note being wrong, and also how it may be put right. From a practical and scientific point of view it would hardly be possible to do this if tone were produced by the vocal cords.

The work as here set forth, is as definite and precise as a piece of perspective drawing.

Thus we are brought into line with the axiom expressed by Herbert Spencer, ' To every art there is a science ' ; our work is put upon a scientific basis, and its votaries considerably gain thereby, for they ' sing with the understanding.' What ' understanding,' or shall we say intelligence, can there be when vocal training is carried on according to the ideas expressed by Mr. David Taylor in the preface of his book, *The Psychology of Singing*. He says:

The only purpose of this work is to demonstrate the falsity of the idea of mechanical vocal management, and to prove the scientific soundness of instruction by imitation. There is no possibility of a practical manual of instruction in singing being accepted, based on the training of the ear and the musical education of the singer, until the vocal world has been convinced of the error of the mechanical idea. When that has been accomplished this work will have served its purpose.

Imitation is, doubtless, of considerable value in the interpretation of music, but the voice itself must first be formed before a satisfactory rendering of any song can be given. There are many artistic people who are not executive artists, because, through lack of technical training and physical control, they have never been able to express what is in their mind.

If the reader will now kindly turn to Figures 3 and 19, some hints can be given which will enable the earnest student to gain such physical control. The advice which we are about to offer is founded, it will be noticed, upon anatomical facts ; and, as

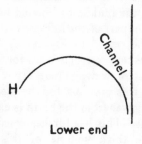

' perfect Nature does nothing in vain,' it will not surprise the student of Nature to know that by working on these lines, results which had been previously pronounced unattainable have been produced ' as if by enchantment.'

The first point to notice, then, is the peculiar manner in which the inferior turbinated bone *H* is tilted. At its lower end, marked *B* (Figure 19), it is so fixed as to form a small channel or groove, whilst, at its upper end, marked *A*, it falls downwards at once, instead of rising upwards first, as it does at its lower end. The obtuse angle which it forms at one end, is thus exactly the reverse of the acute angle which is formed at the other end.

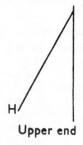

Upper end

Now it seemed to me that such an arrangement could not possibly be a mere matter of chance ; there must be some meaning in it, and use for it. After some deliberation it occurred to me that the use of the channel at the lower end might be to keep in shape and to direct the column of air into the infundibulum (just behind the middle turbinated bone marked *X N*, Figures 3 and 19) which leads to the frontal sinus.

A comparison with Figure 6 may probably help the student to realize this. In Figure 19 the infundibulum cannot be shown because it is behind the middle turbinated bone, but the connection between the after part of the inferior turbinated bone and the infundibulum can be traced in Figure 6. This detail is a fine instance of the perfection of mechanism for voice when regarded from the sinus point of view. There is no need for a physical control of the air at this position, for the movement is automatic when the directing power from the brain is exercised upon the air in the required sinus. This has further consideration in Chapter V, and also in the third volume of this series, *Sinus Tone Production*. The practical lesson to be learned from this figure is the incorrectness and consequently the foolishness of allow- ing the vocal student to think of vocal sounds a b o v e as being termed ' high,' and vocal sounds of a deeper tone as being termed ' low.' The word ' height' as used in ordinary conversation is not applicable to voice. We

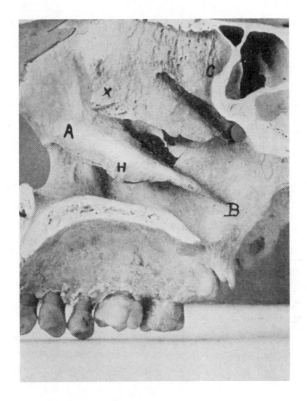

FIGURE 19. TURBINATED BONES—SIDE VIEW

think of the third floor of a building as being higher up than the first floor, and the first floor as being higher than the ground floor ; consequently a vocalist has, consciously or unconsciously, a feeling of rising in getting from that is to say, a perpendicular movement is attempted.

The late John Kennedy in his little book, *Common Sense and Singing*,[1] deals with the subject in a manner which can hardly be regarded as satisfactory. He says, ' Sing an ascending scale with the notes, printed or imagined, inverted to the eye : call up your imaginative faculty, and try all you can to sing down instead of up. Sing your descending scale upwards. Sing an upward interval as if its second note were, in fact, the lower in pitch.'

Now the reader will at once see that Mr. Kennedy was to a certain extent giving good advice.

But let us appeal to the ' common sense ' of the reader and ask, is it not rather ridiculous to say that a student is to do one thing, and if he wishes to do it well he must *imagine* he is doing the very reverse of what he is trying to do ? Mr. Kennedy gives as his reason for this advice that the terms ' high ' and ' low ' when applied to sound are misleading, and remarks that ' height and depth do not enter into the composition of sound.'

We agree that these terms are not applicable to vocal sound but venture to think that the following explanation will be more useful because it is not contradictory, but coincides with anatomical facts.

By reference to Figure 19 it will be seen that the position at C where the air enters the sphenoid sinus for the creation of low notes is higher than the position at B where the air makes its first definite movement towards the frontal sinus. Thus the air starting its journey towards the frontal sinus where high notes are made is in a lower position than the air at C where the low notes are created. The help which a pupil gains when he understands these facts must be experienced to be realized.

The plan adopted by the author when discussing this matter with a pupil is as follows : First tell the pupil that in singing there are not such things as ' high notes.' Naturally he thinks that either a joke or some foolish statement is being made. In order to demonstrate that this is not the case I hold my right

[1] Published by Joseph Williams, Ltd.

hand above my left and then reverse the positions, explaining that in the first case my right hand was above the left and afterwards the left hand was higher than the right. The next step in the argument is to point out that the

note 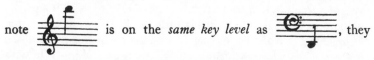 is on the *same key level* as ____, they

do not differ in what is termed ' height.' The correct expression to use would be—the note in the treble clef is a note of *more acute pitch* than that in the bass clef, but certainly not higher. That being settled put some music on the piano desk and find a place where a leap of some interval is made, say for instance Ask the pupil if the second note is higher than the first. The answer of course should be, ' Yes, it is higher,' for clearly the second is above the first. Now take the music from the piano desk and place it flat on a table or the top of the piano and ask : 'Is the second note higher than the first now ? ' The correct reply would be, ' No, it is now on the same level but further forward,' and that, I proceed to explain, is exactly the position which the second note has in your head, namely, further towards the frontal sinus. Hence the movement for scale passages must be a horizontal one instead of perpendicular.

If the teacher follows these suggestions he will, I think, be carrying out the following excellent advice given by Mr. Kennedy, although he hardly carries it out himself. He says : ' Every term he (that is, the teacher) employs should be closely criticized as to its possible effect on the pupil's mind. Enthusiasm, that nothing can damp, must inspire a teacher, but Reason, that nothing can blind, must be its constant attendant.'

The late Sir Arthur Thomson, in writing about common sense in his valuable book, *Introduction to Science*, says : ' By common sense is usually meant the consensus of public opinion, of unsystematic everyday thinking, the untrustworthiness of which is notorious, or the verdict of uncritical sensory experience which has so often proved fallacious.[1] It was common sense that kept the planets circling round the earth ; it was common sense that refused to accept Harvey's demonstration of the

[1] See quotation on page 155 from *Musical Standard*.

circulation of the blood.' It would appear to be the same kind of ' common sense ' which keeps the human voice chained to the vocal cords.

Surely, we would repeat, it is not reasonable to tell a pupil to sing an ascending scale and to try and imagine that the scale is going down. But it does appeal to the reason of both a child and an adult to give an illustration of a see-saw, with pitch of note at one end and position of note at the other. One might even carry the illustration further, and remark that if anyone were to try and bring both ends of a see-saw either up or down at the *same* time, the plank must inevitably snap. So must a voice be damaged, if pitch and position rise or fall at the same time.

' In character, in manner, in style, in all things,' says the poet Longfellow, ' the supreme excellence is simplicity.' Surely these suggestions and facts carry out this ' supreme excellence.'

' But how difficult is it,' wrote Dr. William Harvey to John Riolan, Jun., ' to teach those who have no experience the things of which they have not any knowledge by their senses ! ' So, many men have been content to put this whole work on one side, as being the idea of a ' faddist.' But a simple negation does not prove anything, and I will say, as Dr. Harvey said of his work : ' Whatever may be objected to it by good and learned men, without abusive or contemptuous language, I shall be ready to listen to—I shall even be most grateful to anyone who will take up and discuss the subject,' because, by these means the benefits which are obtainable under the system are more likely to be known. Doctor John Wolcot (' Peter Pindar ') expresses a similar thought in delightful language :

> The sages say, Dame Truth delights to dwell—
> Strange mansion !—at the bottom of a well.
> Questions are then the windlass and the rope
> That pull the grave old gentlewoman up.

An idea which has been found very useful in the early stages of voice training is that of sewing on a metal or pearl button. The inexperienced person having taken the button and placed it upon the material, would put the needle on the reverse side with the intention of getting it through one of the holes with which the button is pierced. Being inexperienced, it is highly improbable that he would at first succeed. He would therefore withdraw the needle and try another place, and perhaps another, until at length

E

the needle being placed exactly at the correct spot, it slips through.
No amount of pressure would get the needle through if it were
wrongly placed, but if the pressure on the button itself were
continued, the result probably would be a broken needle, perhaps
a cut finger. So if the column of air be wrongly directed when
attempting to produce tone (that is, to draw the breath out of the
sinuses), any pressure that is brought to bear upon it will only
result in disaster ; but if it be rightly guided, the sound will *at
once* be produced, because the breath simply slips around the
sinuses, instead of being jammed against them.

In order that the pupil may fully realize how easy is the production of tone, let him take a full inhalation, then gradually
breathe out through the mouth. It will be quite apparent that
there is no physical work in thus quietly letting the breath go, and
there should not be even the smallest amount of added effort in
producing tone, because the only difference between the two is
that, in the first case, the breath coming up from the lungs takes
its first exit, *i.e.*, out of the mouth ; but in the second case—in the
production of tone—the breath is passed through the head and
afterwards out of the nose. The one should be quite as free as the
other.

It might help the student to look upon singing as *negative* work.
That is to say, the only work required is so to control the muscles
that not one of them shall start or jerk. If this be accomplished,
there will not be anything to interfere with the even flow of the
breath from the lungs to the sinuses.

Had the late Mr. Charles Lunn realized the connection which
the sinuses have with the lungs and windpipe, he would
undoubtedly have been even more successful than he was in his
teaching, and his name would probably have been handed down
to posterity as a second Porpora. In his chapter, ' Reinforcement,'
he says : ' Common sense tells us that as Nature has cut off all
ingress to the higher caverns, the one above the uvula should be
cut off too.' Had he studied the anatomy of the head as closely
and thoroughly as he had examined the vocal cords, he could
never have made such a statement. Nature has not cut off the
higher caverns ; they are in direct communication with the lungs.
This one error naturally led to others, and caused many to doubt
the correctness of his teaching, notwithstanding the immense
amount of good which it contained, *e.g.* ' There must be no force

and no effort;' ' Never study for compass;' ' A true vocalist *knows*
but does not *feel* he is singing;' ' Never study short notes until
secure of long ones ; ' ' Never study *crescendo* and *diminuendo*
until tones are fixed.' The directions and statements sometimes
given can, however, hardly be called illuminating. What can we
understand by ' Smashed air in the mouth gives our Anglican
hue;' ' Falsetto is a feigned voice;' ' True falsetto is a whistle
through the false cord, the true cords not acting ' ?

Now the false vocal cords are a very slight elevation, in position
a trifle above the true vocal cords.[1] We have hardly any control
over them, and being, comparatively speaking, some little distance
apart, we might just as well talk about whistling with an open
mouth as whistling through the false cords. Then what is falsetto ?
Falsetto is making use of the air, in the frontal sinuses only and
directing it downwards via the infundibulum. This method
of course will produce only a very thin tone, the larger voice
cavities not being in use ; but the biggest possible tone can be
developed from it when the student has learned how to make
a crescendo and how gradually to bring the other sinuses into
combined use with the frontal. Mr. Lunn says, and quite
correctly, that falsetto ' is rarely used by an artiste except as a
makeshift.' Yet, for all that, an immense amount of good work
can be done by practising ' falsetto ' ; and it is only when the
student is able to develop his falsetto into a full round tone that
he can claim to be anything even approaching a finished singer.
Doubtless there will be many who disagree with these statements
with respect to ' falsetto,' but in this case it is certain that they
cannot have attempted to attain any results from this particular
style of singing. They have only heard it in the undeveloped state
(that being the state referred to by Mr. Lunn), and not liking
it, have discarded it as useless.

In like manner, a person unacquainted with precious stones
would certainly throw away as valueless a diamond, no matter
how large, if he saw it in the rough state. It needs experience to
appraise and understand the value both of the rough stone and
the ' falsetto ' voice ; neither can the value of either of them be
learned in a week or a month.

Madame Lilli Lehmann, in her book, *How to sing*,[2] says :

[1] See Figure 28, facing page 115.
[2] Published by Macmillan & Co., Ltd.

' Most male singers—tenors especially—consider it beneath them, generally, indeed, unnatural or ridiculous, to use the falsetto, which is a part of all male voices. . . . They do not understand how to make use of its assistance. . . .' Of its proper application they have not the remotest conception.'

Mr. E. Davidson Palmer, Mus. Bac., makes some excellent remarks on this subject in his little *Manual of Voice Training*.[1] He says :

The term ' falsetto ' is a most misleading one, and its indiscriminate use has been mischievous in the extreme. The man who invented it has much to answer for. He has caused right to be mistaken for wrong, and wrong to be mistaken for right. He has made what is false appear to be true, and what is true appear to be false. Had it been his supreme desire to do all the injury in his power to the male voices of his own and succeeding generations, he could not, by the exercise of the utmost ingenuity, have devised means better calculated to accomplish his purpose. . . . *The way to get rid of falsetto is to use it.* Let it alone, and it will assuredly remain. It may grow weaker, but so long as voice of any kind remains, it will never disappear. Use it judiciously and perseveringly, and in course of time it will lose its falsetto character and become firm and sonorous. It will then no longer sound strange and artificial, but will have the true manly quality, and will seem to be what it really is, the natural voice. Wherever a separate falsetto register exists, it, and it alone, is the rightly-produced voice. Its extreme high notes, however, are not the notes to practise upon.

Mr. Palmer need not have confined his remarks to male voices, for the whole of the statement is equally applicable to female voices.

Another writer on this subject, M. Martels, must be quoted, for he arrived at conclusions which appear to have been wonderfully near to the whole truth.   Dr. Holbrook Curtis, in dealing with ' The Registers of the Human Voice,' says that in the opinion of the writer Martels, ' notes in the falsetto are in reality *flute* sounds, and that they are not the result of vibrations of the cords proper, but of the air in the cavities above.' Again, Bennati, in his *Mémoire sur le Mécanisme de la Voix pendant le Chant* (Paris, 1832), expresses himself in a somewhat similar manner. He says that ' high notes are not produced in the larynx, but altogether above it.'

Each of these four authors writes well, and with very much truth, regarding the so-called ' falsetto.' It is true that they are dogmatic rather than scientific, but their dogmatism is correct.

[1] Published by Joseph Williams, Ltd.

The whole voice should be developed from 'falsetto,' or, as I should prefer to call it, just that tiny column of air which can be simply *breathed* down the head ; then upon that tone the whole of the superstructure of the voice is built. When this plan is generally followed there will no longer be a dearth of good tenor voices, neither will the voices that are produced last merely one or two seasons, but they will continue for many years in freshness, purity, and beauty. There is no reason why they should not so continue, because the bone which forms the musical instrument will not wear out, although its composition changes. The constituents of bone in a child show a preponderance of animal matter over earthy, whereas in aged people the reverse is the case. The bones will thus contain less vitality, and therefore, there will not be an equal brilliance of tone ; but the muscular part of the machine, not having been strained and put to improper use, will retain its vigour and strength and do with complete ease the only work that should be required of it, viz., the *directing* of the air column. For this reason we would suggest that 'Breath-Governors' would be a better and less misleading name for the so-called 'vocal cords'; as 'breath governors' does describe the work they actually perform.

The acceptance of the work and system contained in this chapter will give the *result* known as 'bel canto' in Italian phraseology ; but it will also mean the dying out of the so-called 'Old Italian System' of training—a 'shibboleth' and a stock phrase used by the learned and the unlearned alike, simply because no one knows exactly what it really means. We know, of course, that the great Italian, Porpora, was the most successful trainer of voices that the world has ever known, but no one knows of any 'system' which he devised. The great painter, James Whistler, said that one 'might as well talk of English mathematics as of English art.'[1] In like manner it is equally ridiculous to speak of an 'Italian method' of vocalization.

The laws of acoustics and the facts of anatomy, on which this book is founded, are the same in all parts of the world ; neither is there any special beauty of tone, or weakness in tone-production, which is peculiar to any country. Nearly every civilized nation can boast of its excellent vocalists, and likewise every country has its would-be singers with 'throaty,' 'nasal,' or 'thin' tone.

[1] Appendix D, page 164.

Let us more fully realize what *is* tone, and then singing, and
good singing, will become more the rule than the exception, and
perhaps some people may remember that an Englishman in the
twentieth century strove hard and earnestly to put the art on a
sure and true foundation.

The *Daily Telegraph*[1] in an excellent article entitled ' The
Reward of Research,' states : ' It has been pointed out by foreign
writers, at least as often as by our own, that Great Britain stands
above all other countries in respect of the number of original and
world-important ideas and discoveries contributed to science.'
The writer hopes and believes that one day this volume will take
its place amongst that number, and so take a small share in proving
that our country can also take an honourable place in the musical
world.

' Musicus ' states in the *Daily Telegraph* for 9th October 1920
that in a letter he has received from the U.S.A. the opinion is
expressed ' that as the musical world is governed, aye and manned
by Russian and German and other Orientals, the Anglo-Saxon of
either British or American stock must finally realize that he or
she must take more or less a back seat.' If we strive, and put our
shoulders to the wheel with sincerity perhaps the seat may be found
not so very far ' back.'

[1] 3rd March 1920.

CHAPTER III

VOCAL CORD TONE PRODUCTION

Popular opinion is the greatest lie in the world.—CARLYLE

IT HAS been said that the medical men of this country prefer 'not to be associated with anything thought cranky.' Under many, and perhaps even most circumstances, such a statement may be true. It will be remembered that William Harvey was put down as a ' crank ' by his fellows ; whilst the surgeons of the forties hated James Simpson for discovering the value of chloroform ; and it was only after the anaesthetic had been used upon Queen Victoria that the ill-founded prejudice against it was broken down.

A few years later, Sir James Simpson himself, after all he had suffered from the prejudice of his brethren, yet was unable to preserve an open and fair-minded judgment upon new thought. For when Dr. Lister came along with his truly marvellous discovery of antiseptic surgery, a discovery which has saved thousands, and probably millions, of people from cruel death, Simpson was one of his most determined and unbending opponents.[1]

It is, therefore, quite evident that the discouragement which was meted out to Roger Bacon for his discoveries in the thirteenth century is by no means merely a medieval blunder. Sir George Stokes (President of the Royal Society) and Professor Huxley have each been guilty of very serious short-sightedness in condemning most important discoveries in the realm of science.

Now, although the word ' guilty ' is used here, let it not be thought that the term is used in a condemnatory sense, but rather to show that although these men were in the foremost rank of advanced thought, yet even they were not always capable of grasping the truth. It has been well stated that ' critics are apt to be meticulously observant, not comprehensively perceptive ; to be occupied with details, and to miss the general aspect.' Thus we see that, however difficult it may be to find the truth, it is often equally, and perhaps more difficult to get it recognized.

[1] Appendix E, page 165.

Perhaps the explanation of this fact may be found in the following remark by Dr. Bretland Farmer : ' Nature only speaks to those who know how to listen, and how to question ; but those who have once learnt this lesson have thereby obtained possession of a key to knowledge that will fit many locks and disclose the secret of many mysteries.'

Let not the reader lose sight of these introductory remarks, as we go on and consider the capabilities of the vocal cords as sound producers, and endeavour to ascertain how far such a theory is in accordance with scientific and acoustic laws. At the outset, it would perhaps be well to explain that the term ' cords ' is slightly misleading. The cords are not free in the same way that they are in a piano or violin, but they are connected along their whole length to the thyroid cartilages and only their inner edges are free. Although this should be borne in mind, it will not in the least disturb the validity of the facts which we are about to mention.

In the first place, then, a cord of any sort whatever must of necessity be stretched and strained to a degree that approaches breaking point if it is to produce sound, especially a sound which is high in pitch. Dr. Holbrook Curtis informs us that ' to make the purest initial tone from the cords, we must get the utmost possible tension.' Surely it is quite inconceivable that any part of our anatomy should have to be placed in such a position before it can be made to answer the purpose for which it exists. Yet we are by physical laws bound to believe that such a strain does take place— if the vocal cords create tone.

In Dr. Aikin's book, *The Voice*,[1] already quoted, the following passage occurs :

It is the law of vibrating strings that the tension increases in proportion to the square of the vibrations. If, then, the vibrations of the lowest note of the compass be taken as 1, the middle note will be 2, and the upper note 4, each one in rising being the double of the other. But the tension increases as the square of the vibrations, so that if the tension is 1, that for the middle note is $2^2=4$, and for the top note of the compass $4^2=16$. As the air pressure follows very much the same proportion as the tension, it will be seen at once that in rising through the scale the increase of tension and pressure required for every higher note is greater and greater the higher we get ; and to add another note to the top of the compass requires no small additional effort.

[1] 1910 edition, published by Longmans & Co.

The law here enunciated is quite correct, and *must* be carried out under existing tenets of vocal cord production.

We need hardly be surprised then, that the *Nineteenth Century and After* should make remarks upon 'getting a spasmodic grip of a handy piece of furniture in order to produce a high note *di bravura*'!

A further detail, however, and one of much importance, is that if the vocal cords (see Figure 20) were so strained, they would without doubt pull the arytenoid cartilages off the cricoid or ring cartilage, on which they rest and move. This statement, originally written by the present author in May 1908, has since been quite independently confirmed by Dr. Marage, of Paris, in a report upon his laryngological observations, which he presented to the Académie des Sciences in November 1909. Commenting upon the experiments of the German scientist, J. Müller, he says :[1] ' Cet expérimentateur n'avait pu obtenir que des vibrations ne rappelant pas du tout celles des larynxes vivants ; et encore tendait-il les cordes vocales avec des forces bien supérieures à celles que peuvent déployer les muscles intralaryngiens (1 kilogramme, parfois) ; ces forces, chez le vivant, auraient arraché les arytenoides.'

The next point for consideration is the fact that a cord for sound production must be hardened and quite dry. Now the vocal cords are certainly not composed of any kind of hardened material, but they are folds of membranous muscular tissue, capable of considerable movement and of much elasticity. Probably everyone knows how difficult and almost impossible it is even to talk with a dry throat, and it is an interesting fact that Nature has endowed the vocal cords with special means for lubrication. On the inner surface, *i.e.*, away from the thin edge, are small cells from which exudes a white fluid which flows on to the edges of the cords and so keeps them always in a moist and supple condition.[2]

Here, then, are two opposite facts—first, that a cord of any sort must be hard and dry in order to produce musical sound ; second,

[1] ' This experimenter had only been able to obtain vibrations which could not be recognized in any way as those of living larynxes ; moreover, he stretched the vocal cords with a force much greater than that which the intralaryngeal muscles could display (1 kilogramme, occasionally) this force upon the living larynx would have torn out the arytenoids.'
[2] Appendix F, page 166.

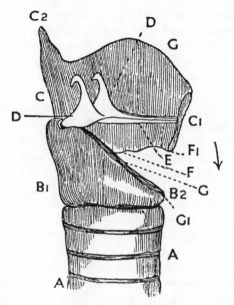

FIGURE 20.   WINDPIPE AND VOCAL CORDS

A A. Windpipe.

B1, B2. Cricoid cartilage forming the upper extremity, or top, of the windpipe.

C, C, C1, C2. One-half or side of the thyroid cartilage. *C1* is that part of the throat known as ' Adam's apple.' The corresponding half of the thyroid cartilage forms an angle at this position. Naturally this half (not shown here) has a horn agreeing with *C2*. On these two points the tongue (or hyoid) bone rests. The *whole* of this cartilage hinges on the cricoid, so that the distance between *B2* and *C1* can be lessened.

This movement is effected by means of muscles known as the crico-thyroid muscles. They stretch from the inner side of the thyroid cartilage at the points *F F1* to the cricoid cartilage at *G G1*. They, of course, continue along the right side of the cartilage also. The muscles are not drawn in the figure, in order that the shape and position of the cartilages may be better shown. Reference is again made to these muscles on pages 105 and 106.

D D. Two arytenoid cartilages, each of which rests upon the edge of the cricoid cartilage.

E. Vocal cord (only one is shown). Fixed at one end to the angle formed by the two thyroid cartilages, and at the other end to the vocal process at the base of the arytenoid cartilage (see Figure 27, page 101). The arytenoid cartilages rotate, the one from right to left, and the other from left to right—that is, *towards* each other, and in so doing carry the vocal cords with them, also towards each other, making thereby a greater or less air space between them.

that the vocal cords are soft and wet. How is it possible to make such opposite truths agree ?

Another point may be noticed from the before-mentioned musical libel case. Sir J. Milsom Rees, the eminent voice specialist, in his evidence, stated that he was aware that ' the plaintiff was teaching singing with the full length of the vocal cord, and he believed it was a great strain for the voice ; although he admitted some of our greatest singers used it.' (Fourth day's trial, 13th February.) Now, if a cord of any sort be set in vibration, surely it must vibrate throughout its *whole* length, unless some definite means be taken to prevent its doing so. Clearly, no cord can stop its own vibration at different points of its length. Yet one of the first and most prominent throat doctors of the day declares that this is what the vocal cords do. If they do so, it is evident that they are a law unto themselves, obeying no principle yet known.

Merely for the sake of being both exact and complete, it is perhaps well to mention the fact that some of the deeper fibres of the inferior portion of the thyro-arytenoid muscle, known as the ' ary vocalis of Ludwig,' are supposed to have the power of making a portion of the vocal cords tense, while the remainder is relaxed. Even if this statement be correct, its practical value must be very small, for it is perfectly clear that a vocalist would be very much at sea if asked to tighten or loosen his ' ary vocalis of Ludwig.' It would also appear that the bare statement must be difficult to prove, for the fibres being deep seated cannot possibly be examined in the living subject during phonation. Therefore the capability claimed might well be taken as a flattering accomplishment to the ' ary vocalis.'

Dr. Aikin has also expressed opinions that coincide with those of Sir J. Milsom Rees. Dr. Aikin says : ' There is, however, another way in which high notes can be produced. When the vocal cords are more tightly pressed together, the vibrations at their back-ends in the neighbourhood of the vocal processes,[1] are interfered with by compression, or " stopped." A high note is thus produced, without increase of tension or air pressure, but the sound is smaller and thinner than that produced by the whole length of the cords.'

In another part of the same work the author says : ' It is not

[1] The vocal processes can be seen in Figure 27, page 101.

necessary in any practical work upon the voice to go closely into all muscular actions in connection with this mechanism, because they are not under the control of the will.'

It will be noticed that both these specialists agree that the vocal cords can vibrate throughout their entire length, or along a section of it only.

As, however, Dr. Aikin admits—and quite correctly—that the muscular actions ' are not under the control of the will ' it is rather difficult to see what practical advantage can be gained by studying the vocal cords, either ' at their back-ends,' or anywhere else. Moreover, as the tone thus produced is, we are told, ' smaller and thinner than that produced by the whole length of the cords,' it could be of no real value to any vocalist, even if it were possible to bring the mechanism under the control of the singer.

Thus we are confronted with three very awkward facts in the theory and practice of vocal cord vocalization.

1. A cord cannot stop its own vibrations at any particular point.

2. We have no control over either the ' ary vocalis ' or ' the back-ends of the vocal cords,' or, indeed, over any separate or single part of their action.

3. Even if these two objections could be overcome—but they cannot—the resulting tone, being ' smaller and thinner,' would be of little practical value.

Again, the shortness of the vocal cords would also certainly indicate an inability to produce one and one-half or two octaves of notes. In women, the cords are about half an inch in length. If, therefore, the usual laws of string vibrations be carried out, there may only be one quarter-inch of vocal cord in use to produce the octave of the lowest note ; and if that quarter-inch be divided into its component parts, according to recognized acoustic laws, we should be driven to some very extraordinary conclusions. In the second volume of *Surgical Anatomy*, by John B. Deaver, M.D.,[1] it is stated : ' The thyroid cartilage, (see Figure 20), is larger in men than in women, so that there is increased length of vocal cord, which has, therefore, in accordance with a well-established law of physics, a lower pitch, thus accounting for the deeper tones of the male.' Now it has already been stated that the average length of vocal cord in women is half an inch ; in men it

[1] Surgeon-in-chief to the German Hospital, Philadelphia.

is usually three-quarters of an inch. Is it then ' in accordance with a well-established law of physics ' that a cord which is lengthened to the extent of *one-half* shall produce a tone which is two octaves lower ? The fact that a bass voice is, roughly speaking, two octaves lower than a soprano, certainly cannot be scientifically accounted for on such a theory, neither have we knowledge of any kind of string which will produce so low a note as with a length of only three-quarters of an inch. Such a note would require a cord of considerable length, density, and thickness, none of which qualities do the vocal cords possess.

Whilst dealing with the length of the vocal cords, we would point out that there is no certain difference between the length of cords in a bass voice and in a tenor. Dr. F. W. Mott, in his interesting book, *The Brain and the Voice in Speech and Song*, says : ' We should also expect a constant difference in the length of the cords of the tenor and bass in the male, and of the contralto and soprano in the female, but such is not the case. . . . The vocal cords may be as long in the tenor as in the bass.'.

The *Daily Mail* for 10th August 1921 contained a short notice upon Signor Caruso, written by Dr. W. Lloyd, F.R.C.S. Therein it was stated that Caruso's vocal cords were one-sixth of an inch longer than those of any other tenor whom the doctor had examined. We have no reason to doubt the correctness of this statement, but if it be true, then his vocal cords should undoubtedly have produced bass notes in accordance with well-known and proved acoustic laws ; whereas we find the longer cords producing higher notes !

Now when we consider that Prof. J. Thomson lays down as a ' *first step in scientific procedure, that all science begins with measurement,*' it is fully evident that we have here yet other instances of the utter hopelessness of making any scientific explanation of vocal tone if it is produced in the larynx.

Prof. Thomson further states that ' *the fundamental postulate of science is the Uniformity of Nature* ' ;[1] a fact to which vocal professors give no heed. A little time since, a well-known tutor was trying to show me that my system was incorrect. In reply I said, ' There is nothing in the world which, with a length of only half an inch, can produce two octaves of tone.' ' No,' said he,

---

[1] Prof. Thomson's italics in each case.

' there is not, *except* the vocal cords.' Thus he placed the vocal cords in a category entirely by themselves, separated from everything in the known universe, utterly regardless of the fact that Uniformity of Nature is the first postulate of science.

John Stuart Mill wrote : ' Everything in Nature pursues an invariable order. The same antecedents were followed by the same consequents, always and everywhere '—a truth which *Musical News*, 3rd May 1913, well expressed as follows : ' The Almighty works always in the same . . . . unvarying way.' Can our local professors and our hospital tutors, when dealing with the throat, honestly subscribe to these evident realities ? The quotation from Dr. Mott's book may perhaps indicate that doubts are beginning to rise as to whether all accepted vocal theories are really in quite good order. Be that as it may, we will continue our argument still further.

To produce tone with a string it must either be struck, plucked, or drawn by a roughened bow of hair. It is of course quite clear that our vocal cords can neither be struck, plucked or scraped. Anyone who plays a bowed instrument knows how necessary the resin is for a satisfactory performance, because without it the hair would not grip the string. It would probably not require much argument to convince the reader that it would be highly undesirable either to grip or to hit his vocal cords, even if it were possible.

Thus we have here yet another point which will prove an awkward detail to explain satisfactorily, if the larynx is to continue to hold supremacy in the world of vocalization.

Again, Dr. Marage gives independent support to my views. In the report already quoted he states :[1] ' En aucun cas les lois des vibrations des cordes ne m'ont paru s'appliquer aux vibrations des cordes vocales ; celles-ci n'ont pas de son par elles-mêmes, c'est l'air qui vibre.'

On page 25 it was stated—and the fact can easily be proved—that in singing a *crescendo* passage the louder tone is produced by the vocal cords separating and so allowing a larger column of air to pass between them. Suppose now a singer is producing a single note with a *crescendo*. By the time that the full tone is

---

[1] In no case have the laws of the vibrations of cords appeared to me to apply to the vibrations of the vocal cords ; these latter have *no* sound by themselves, it is the air which vibrates.

reached, the cords will be wider apart than at starting. This means that there absolutely *must* be a different tension upon them. Yet the singer is producing a note of exactly the same pitch, although the tension of the cord has altered. If the vocal cords really produce sound, our scientists will have to seek for some fresh law or laws to explain the possibility of such an extraordinary occurrence as cords with an increasing tension producing exactly the same pitch. If, on the other hand, they do not produce sound, there is nothing which calls for any comment, for they merely separate in order to allow more breath to pass between them up to the voice cavities.

Professor Tyndall, in one of his lectures on sound, states that tone is created in the larynx by the vibrations of the vocal cords, and that the higher sounds are produced by their greater tension. Yet anyone who can use the laryngoscope can see for himself what happens in a *crescendo* passage. Starting a single note *piano*, the cords are close together; as the tone increases, the larger column of air which is coming upwards from the lungs pushes the cords further apart and from this position ‖ they assume more the shape of a curve.

Now it is perfectly clear that when the two ends of a cord are fixed, so far as a forward movement is concerned,[1] there must be a greater tension upon it when describing a curve than when in a straight line. Thus, according to all known laws, the cords being tighter should be producing a higher note. But they are not doing so. The same note is being sung, but in a louder tone. We may continue the same line of thought further and note that the vocal cords are widest apart, thus ( ), and therefore at a still higher tension in deep breathing, when they produce no sound at all.

Although not generally known, yet it is a further fact, and one of much import, that with the vocal cords thus wide apart, it is quite possible to sing either sustained notes or simple scale-passages.

Surely these truths show us that theory and practice are not altogether in harmony. Well may Dr. Guillemin write in his book, *Génération de la Voix et du Timbre*: 'Les théories actuelles sont un tissu de contradictions, et il n'y a rien à en tirer.'[2]

---

[1] The movement of the arytenoid cartilages which hold one end of the cords is chiefly rotary.

[2] The existing theories are a tissue of contradictions and there is nothing to be deduced from them.

It is quite certain that there is but one function which the vocal cords should be required to perform, and that is to govern and direct the amount of air which passes upwards through the head, and the formation of the cords themselves is quite in accordance with the statement, for they are not, as their name might imply, rounded ligaments, but three-cornered, thus A $\triangledown\triangleright$ A. The sides A A are, as already stated, connected with the thyroid cartilage, whilst the inner edges come towards each other in phonation. It can be readily understood that a column of air coming upwards from below could be well formed by them into a jet and so directed to any required spot.

An excellent simile is found in water issuing from a garden hose. Should the end of the pipe be void of any metal fittings, the water will travel but a short distance, and be very little under control ; but let a person take the free end of the pipe and nearly close the rubber by pressing the fingers round it, then a small jet of water is made which can easily be directed at will. Another suggestion will also help to drive home the point. Take an ordinary specimen vase, and direct a column of air towards the top of it with the lips. If the lips direct the air properly a musical note is the result ; but the lips do not make the sound. Afterwards, with the mouth wide open, direct the breath towards the vase, and there will be no sound at all. The lips here answer for the vocal cords, and the vase for the sinus in the head. When the vocal cords are wide apart there is no sound, but when we sing or speak, they come together and direct the air column towards the head.

In the course of his studies, the writer has ascertained an interesting fact of much practical value, which bears directly upon this matter. It is that the vocal cords are much closer together when a true, bright tone is sung than when a ' breathy ' tone is produced.

How exactly this corresponds with the simile of the garden hose ! We know that if the water passes out through a small hole it will travel a greater distance, and, therefore, would hit any object in its course with greater force, than if it came through a large opening. So it is with the air-column and the vocal cords. When the vocal cords are close together the air column is better focussed and more compact, and, therefore, naturally can produce a better tone.

Let the cords separate a little, and the moving column is less under control, with the result that part of the air escapes by way of the mouth, whilst the remainder in a feeble manner finds its way through the sinuses.

But, it may be asked, where is the promised *practical* value ? It lies in the fact that the so-called ' open throat '—the cherished idea of many and many a professor—is shown to be wrong.

I can quite imagine the vigorous and emphatic denunciation which such a doctrine is likely to receive from many of my brethren. But be it observed, I am not advising a tight throat or the slightest fixity of muscles. I merely point out what anyone can see, providing he can use the laryngoscope, viz., the physical fact that the vocal cords are further apart when a bad, breathy tone is produced than they are when singing a true, bright note. In neither case need the muscles be either set or strained.

One of the greatest difficulties in the art of singing is that of overcoming this tendency to tighten, and, by so doing, to prevent the vocal cords from doing more than their proper share of the work.

The first obstruction which the air column meets in the outward passage is the vocal cords, and directly they feel any air pressure their natural tendency is to tighten. This is precisely what has to be avoided, and it is due to the non-avoidance of this essential particular that ' nodes ' form on the cords, throats get ' relaxed,' and many other evils arise.

Exactly the same law is carried out in every other part of our anatomy. If we overtax our digestive organs we get indigestion and many attendant evils. If we do too much reading our eyesight suffers. If we do too much writing with stiffened fingers we get ' writer's cramp.' So if we stiffen the muscles of the larynx and overburden them with work, a penalty has to be paid. Of course, the difficulty is to keep them free, but it is a similar difficulty which is experienced by the swordsman in learning to fence, by the billiard-player in handling his cue, as well as by the pianist in controlling his fingers, viz., the utmost relaxity and freedom of all the muscles.

When, however, the vocal student realizes that sound is absolutely *made* in the head, then it is a comparatively easy matter to keep all the muscular part of the throat in a state of complete ease and freedom.

The illustration of a leaky tap has sometimes been found useful

F

in helping the pupil to start the tone with absolute freedom of muscles. The pupil is shown that the water simply falls from the tap by its own weight, and not by any pressure from behind it. Then he can carry out the idea by letting the breath slide away, as it were, from the sinuses without any upward pressure from the lungs below.[1] This having been accomplished, and the sinuses cleared of all superabundant mucus (which when present must necessarily deaden sound), then the singer is in possession of Nature's full vocal powers, and providing the artistic instinct is also present, then are the hearers charmed and thrilled with the exquisite pathos, the invigorating energy, or the delightful happiness which only the human voice and mind combined can display.

Unfortunately, tutors as a body, do not realize that the physical development of a pupil is a matter quite apart from the poetical, just as much as one's dress is a thing apart from one's food. The student is usually given some book of vocalizes, the melodies of which are pretty enough and quite interesting, but utterly useless for the purpose of voice development. A dozen of them all put together would never teach a learner how to use his voice, or where to place it, or how to proceed in order to control it. A master with a fairly good voice tells his pupil to sing a note or a phrase in the same tone or manner as he has just done. The pupil tries his utmost, but not knowing exactly how the said phrase was produced, naturally fails in his attempt to copy his tutor, who, being equally ignorant of the physical cause of the difference between the two renderings—although he hears it clearly enough—is unable to put his pupil into position for the right sound. The attempt is made again and again, with a worse result each time, unless the learner by blind chance happens to light upon the correct position. Thus matters go from bad to worse, and the pupil is at length given up, or, as is more probably the case, retires voluntarily, as not having sufficient ' ability.'

An endorsement of this sad state of affairs appeared in the *Musical Times* for April 1910. The article is headed, ' Italian Singing Teaching,' and is a translation and digest of two articles signed ' R. C.' (Romeo Carugati), which appeared in the *Lombardia*, a Milanese newspaper. The *Musical Times* says :

Mr. Carugati's experiences and deductions are certainly amusing and deplorable, and not a little instructive. He sheds a lurid light on

[1] Compare this with page 38 and Figure 18.

the conditions of voice-training prevailing—to an extent, at any rate—in Milan, and the note of warning he sounds should not go unheeded. The principal title of his article is ' The Market of Voices.'

' We have voices in Italy,' begins the writer, ' our language itself is music, but we lack lyrical artists . . . The old robust voices capable of resistance, and all-powerful, are no more . . . . exceptions are very rare. . . . There are 200 or more teachers of singing in Milan ; about ten of them deserve that name, and they are, perhaps, not the best known. . . . The competition is the greatest possible. Those especially who come with illusions from abroad are confronted by people ready to make the most wonderful promises of easy and speedy success. The poor students pass from master to master, and the final result is complete loss of voice.'

So much for the average Italian voice-training.

In the quarterly *Music and Letters*, for July 1920, Mr. Walter Ford has a very interesting article, ' Some thoughts on Singing.' After pointing out the very considerable improvement that has taken place in the writing of vocal music, he continues :

There is another side to the picture to which it is folly not to turn our eyes. . . . In reaching forward to higher ideals of song on its musical and interpretative side we have gradually been dropping the high ideal that used to prevail on the technical side. As craftsmen we have gone down no less steadily than as musicians we have gone up. The horizon has narrowed in the one direction in proportion as it has broadened in the other. We sing more songs and better, but our voices are less good, less cunning, and alas, less durable.

Mr. Ford's opinion is thoroughly upheld and endorsed in the *Daily Telegraph* for 31st May 1921. On that date ' Musicus ' writes as follows :

It is not so very long ago that, when it was pointed out in this page that one of the detriments to a perfect representation of the lighter forms of opera was the scarcity of singers sufficiently accomplished in the particular way requisite, a huge mass of correspondence poured in from all and sundry contradicting every word that was said. Well, nothing much seems to have happened in the meantime. But it is rather significant, is it not, that Mr. Henry Savage is urging in the United States of America the scarcity we complained of ? I read that, ' his musical director has heard several hundreds of applicants, and found less than a dozen who have good voices and the requisite singing ability.' Well, is not that, roughly speaking, precisely what was said here only a few months ago ? The point is that there are myriads of singers who think themselves ' good enough,' but when tried there is the indefinable something missing. But it is terribly sad that both England and America should be found to have a scarcity in this commodity just at one and the same moment.

It must of course be admitted that we have both at home and abroad many excellent singers of talent and merit who might combine to form a picture of great optimism in the matter. Their numbers, however, would certainly not be legion, whilst there are hundreds and probably thousands who would entirely agree with the opinions held and demonstrated by Mr. Carugati, Mr. Ford, ' Musicus,' and others. It has been well said, ' Of singers that fail, more fail from want of proper direction than from want of voice.'

There is not the slightest doubt as to the truth of this statement ; and what is the cause—what is really at the very root—of this ' want of proper direction ' ? Is it that the tutors are themselves lazy and take no interest in their work ? I am certain this is not the case, for very few people would embark upon a musical career unless they really felt a love for the art and an interest in it, and therefore a keen desire to see their pupils improve.

The true explanation of the dilemma is to be found in the fact that it is exceedingly difficult to find a professor of singing who realizes that the voice has to be gradually and slowly developed, simply note by note. It does not occur to the average teacher that the first step towards vocal control should consist in directing the pupil to listen keenly to the tones which he himself is producing, so that he may detect any variation, however slight, in quality or power.

The usual object in voice-training is to get through as many vocalizes as possible, with the addition, perhaps, of a few scales and *arpeggi*, in the hope that by merely singing these the voice will be strengthened and developed. If the voice happens to be one which is naturally well placed, this hope may probably be more or less fulfilled. But if the singer starts with a small amount of what is termed ' natural ability,' only too frequently throat troubles come along, and the would-be singer retires with his hopes blighted and his purse lighter.

After all, there is but little discredit to the master under these circumstances, and certainly still less to the pupil, for each has really done his best. The fault is in the system of vocal cord tone production, wherein, to some extent,—and sometimes, to a large extent—the voice is left to take care of itself, while the student merely learns a certain number of melodies in the fond hope and firm belief that by energetically singing these his voice is sure to improve.

The course adopted in Sinus Tone Production is absolutely different. Here he is taught *how* to produce his notes. His attention is directed to the many various points which combine to make the difference between good tone and bad ; and, with practice, he can detect the smallest variation in the quality of the tone which he is producing, and having learned to control the different sinuses, he is able to increase or lessen at will the proportion or balance of tone which proceeds from each. Thus he not only knows what he wants, but he is the happy possessor of a clear and definite knowledge as to how he can get it.

The compass of the voice is dealt with in an equally precise and careful manner. Different vowel and consonant sounds have each assigned to them their own particular range of notes for practice ; and, as the vocal machine develops, so these directions are altered, and the pupil's voice extends semitone by semitone, until at length its full compass and power are reached. Thus the sound—that is to say, the tone which constitutes the voice—is itself built up step by step, and the owner thereof is absolute master of it in every detail.

One of the difficulties which the pupil finds in attaining this mastery, is the new sensation experienced in spacing out the voice —so to speak. In the vocal cord system, the whole range of the voice must be produced in a space of $\frac{3}{4}$ of an inch, that being the length of the male vocal cord, hence there can be no possible freedom of movement. In Sinus Tone Production there is a length of about three inches from the sphenoid sinus to the frontal, the whole of which is brought into use. Compare $\frac{3}{4}$ of an inch——————— with three inches———————————————————————— and it will be readily understood that it takes a little time to get used to the change which is entailed in finding the vocal machine quadrupled in size.[1] It is however, a joy to know that in many and probably most cases, the capabilities of the voice increase in the same ratio by the change in method of training.

An American writer, Mr. J. Van Brockhoven, issued in 1908 a book named *The True Method of Tone Production*, in which he advances some ingenious ideas designed to show that the vocal cords do not produce sound. He says :

How can the thin edges of two bundles of muscles known as the vocal cords, by vibrating, produce one absolutely pure tone identical in pitch

---

[1] This matter is dealt with more fully in the third book of this series *Sinus Tone Production*.

and quality ?   How can the mere edge of a bundle of muscles forming a curve or concave line be strung sufficiently tense to produce a tone by the vibration of the curved edge?   How can the whole singing range of the male and female voice . . . be produced by the vibration of the thin edge of the two vocal cords not even one inch in length ?

After further arguments he continues : ' My own personal investigations established the hitherto unknown fact that the process of producing tone on a trumpet has its counterpart in the vocal organ.' He then draws a parallel between the mouth-piece of a trumpet and the true and false vocal cords with the laryngeal pouch[1] (technically known as the sacculus laryngis).

His theories, however, will not stand examination, for, in the first place, it is more than doubtful if the false vocal cords can move in the manner he describes, and if they can, it is hardly probable that they could produce such a shaped pocket as would constitute the cavern which, in Mr. Van Brockhoven's opinion, is responsible for sound. However, for the sake of argument, we will suppose that all these matters are possible and quite correct, and that such changes as the illustrations which his book shows can take place. Still there are two facts which alone are sufficient to disprove the whole scheme.

The first is : In Dr. Cunningham's *Text Book of Anatomy* it is stated : ' The false vocal cords are of little importance with respect to voice . . . indeed, they can in great part be destroyed and no appreciable difference in the voice result.'[2]

The second is : That the mouthpiece of a trumpet is composed of hard polished metal, whilst the pocket or cavity formed at the position of the upper (false) cords is of very soft, pliant, and yield-ing tissue, and therefore quite incapable of *generating* sound. It would appear therefore that the ' personal investigations ' of our American author must take their place on the shelf with those ideas which the *Daily Telegraph* (18th August 1920) terms ' half-baked discoveries and unverified deductions.'

Two scientific details which are not in this category can be found in the study of hydrogen gas, and also of oxygen. The first—in Carlylean phrase—' is indicative of much.' It consists in the fact that the pitch of an organ pipe and the pitch of the human voice are, in each case, raised by using hydrogen gas instead

[1] See Figure 28 facing page 115 and Figure 29 on page 119.
[2] This fact is a serious blow to some of the theories held by the late Mr. Charles Lunn.

of ordinary air; whilst the pitch of a violin or a tuning fork is unaffected by the gas. If voices were produced by the greater or less tension of the vocal cords, then hydrogen gas would have no effect upon the number of vibrations, as with the violin. The fact that hydrogen causes the voice to rise in pitch distinctly goes to endorse the theories contained in this volume, that the human voice is purely a wind instrument.

The lesson from oxygen gas is not of so much importance, although it is certainly worth consideration. In a book, *The Basic Law of Vocal Utterance*, by Emil Sutro, the author remarks : ' It does not seem reasonable . . . to suppose that the air, after having been deprived of its main component, should be used in its vitiated form to produce sound.' Let us now carefully examine Herr Sutro's statement in the light of scientific knowledge, in the place of his attitude of supposition. It is a fact that nitrogen, which constitutes 79 per cent. of the air, and is, therefore, its main component, remains unchanged by inhalation. Exactly the same amount is expired as was previously inspired. But with respect to oxygen, 20 per cent. of its own volume is lost during inspiration and is changed to carbonic acid gas. Thus the air loses oxygen by inhalation but gains carbonic acid gas.

Now compare this with a statement made by Mr. Valdemar Poulsen in a lecture which he gave upon ' Wireless Telegraphy.' The account will be found in the *Electrician* for 16th November 1906. In speaking of experiments he had been making for the production of atmospheric vibrations, he says : ' Thus, oxygen would appear to be a harmful factor.' So we see that the chemical change which takes place by the body reducing the 20.96 per cent. of oxygen in the inspired air to 16.03 per cent. in the expired air, is really a change which from known science is likely to assist vocalization, and should not, so far as singing is concerned, be termed ' vitiated air.'

Here, then, are many and various arguments that sound is produced by vibrating air, not by vibrating cords, but the vibrations are formed, not, as Mr. Van Brockhoven states, in the laryngeal pouch, but in the head, where there are free air chambers, strong and light, of very thin texture, admirably suited for the purpose I claim for them. Moreover, if the function of these sinuses is not for music and speech, then what possibly can be their use ? I have seen it stated in a medical work : ' The use of

these sinuses is not known ' ; whilst in another work[1] it is stated :
' In the first place, the purpose of these cavities has long been
accepted as that of lessening the weight of the facial bones, but
although obviously air-chambers, their ventilating arrangement
. . . must be held to be imperfect.' Such a passage in a text-book
can hardly be considered satisfactory. It seems to imply that the
theory of ' lessening the weight of the facial bones ' has only ' long
been accepted ' for want of a better reason. This is certainly a
very weak statement, because, if such were their object, it would
be better served by their non-existence. The ' facial bones '
manage very well indeed without the sphenoid sinus for the first
fourteen years of life, so there is certainly no apparent reason why
they should not afterwards continue so to do if the sole duty of
the sinus was the negative one of ' lessening weight.'

It has been quite seriously stated by scientific men,[2] and
accepted by those who have been their pupils, that were these
sinuses solid bone, instead of hollow chambers, the skull would be
too heavy to balance upon the spinal column. Such a proposition
is too ridiculous for any person to accept if he gives himself the
trouble to consider the reasonableness of the argument ; for the
additional weight could only be a few ounces at the most ; yet
porters and men of that class can, and continually do, carry weights
of thirty or forty pounds and more upon their heads, and that
without any discomfort to the spinal column.

The idea of a ' ventilating arrangement ' is equally poor ; and
the work of Nature as exemplified in the human body created ' in
the image of God ' can hardly ' be held to be imperfect.'

Until the seventeenth century, arguments of an equally poor
character were used for many years by physicians in their
endeavour to explain the work done by the valves in the veins ; and
when, after years of hard work and study, William Harvey had
the courage to explain their true office, he was for a considerable
time looked upon as a ' crack-brain,' and treated accordingly.

As a musical instrument, the sinuses, coupled with the remainder
of the machinery, form a perfect whole.

A point of considerable interest, and one which should not be
lost sight of, is the formation of the wall of the cranium and of the

---

[1] *The Throat and Nose and their Diseases*, by Lennox Browne,
F.R.C.S. Edin., Senior Surgeon to the Central Throat and Ear Hospital.
[2] See *Musical Standard*, 9th April 1910.

hard palate which constitutes the floor of the nose. It consists of two layers of compact bony substance, and has an intervening cancellated substance called diploe. (See Figure 21, which is a photograph of a section of the hard palate highly magnified.) By reference to Figures 2 and 3 it will be seen that diploe enters very largely into the composition of the skull. The advantages of such an arrangement are numerous. Firstly, it is known in mechanics that such a disposition of material gives the greatest possible strength with the greatest possible lightness. Secondly, in case of a blow, the diploe acts as a buffer, and so shields the inner layer. Thirdly, and this is the important matter from a musical standpoint, the diploe, with its hundreds of air cells, must certainly form a perfectly ideal tone conductor and resonator. I should think it highly probable that, with respect to the middle and highest registers of the voice, more tone is conducted into the mouth or buccal cavity through the medium of the hard palate than by any other means.

In other words, there are two ways by which the air in the mouth can be set in vibration. One is by communication backwards into the mouth, by way of the dotted line shown in Figure 3 (facing page 17); the other is by the tone column as it comes directly downwards from the infundibulum striking the hard palate, which, being a first-rate resonator, would communicate the vibrations to the air in the mouth. With practice, one can often *feel* the air column in the highest register striking on the hard palate. This is not so noticeable with notes in the low register of the voice, because the air column from the sphenoid sinus does not strike directly downwards upon the hard palate as it does from the frontal sinus, but takes the direction of the line of the probe as shown in Figure 18.

Thus, all high and medium notes come directly downwards from the points indicated at F, X X in Figure 3[1] and make their exit through the nostrils, technically known as the anterior nares.

Let the reader again compare Figures 21 and 3, and he will observe that the overhanging bone at the top of the former plate is the same as that marked H in the latter, and is the inferior turbinated bone which forms the inferior meatus below it. Figure 21 is of special value, not only for giving a splendid idea of the

[1] The exact outlets for the medium notes are just behind the marks X X, on the turbinated bones.

formation of the bone which forms the hard palate, but also for the very clear idea which one can get of the cavernous nature of the inferior meatus and of its consequent suitability as a resonator. The middle and superior meatuses are of course above this one.

It is quite a usual practice for tutors and writers to explain that tone should be brought to the teeth, thus intentionally giving the idea that the column of air should travel through the mouth and hit the teeth at right angles underneath the hard palate. Mr. Charles Tree, in his book, *How to acquire Ease of Voice Production*[1], (which contains much excellent advice), tells his readers ' to push the . . . . vowels to the . . . . spot where the hard palate meets the teeth '; and in another place bids them ' carefully observe how the vowel *ee* brings the vocal tone still a little more forward in the mouth ; brings it right to the front of the hard palate and right on to the teeth.'

In passing we would notice that the vowel *ee* does not invariably ' bring the vocal tone still a little more forward.' There are many people who find that *ee* is liable to send the tone backward. One of the first duties of the voice trainer should be to ascertain what vowels each individual pupil finds the easiest to produce. One student may find a hum help most, another *ou*, another *ah*, and another *ee*. The judgment of the master must determine which sound has the purest and most forward tone. It may be fully granted that as a matter of *sensation only*, the tone may be felt close to the teeth, but as a matter of *fact*, if tone be made by the vocal cords, it is absurd to tell a student to feel it at the teeth, for we have seen (see pages 16 and 18) that breath coming out of the mouth towards the teeth cannot possibly create tone. In an important book entitled *The Science and Practice of Dental Surgery*[2] it is stated : ' The teeth of man also serve as adjuncts in vocalization and in articulate speech.'

In articulate speech the teeth are undoubtedly required, but certainly not in vocalization. Let us consider the matter further. ' To distinguish between appearance and reality—is what the scientific mood seeks after.' The complete jaw-bone is composed of two different kinds of material. The upper part in which the teeth are set is technically known as alveolus. Alveolus is a kind

[1] Published by Joseph Williams, Ltd.
[2] Edited by Norman Bennett, M.A., M.B., B.C. Cantab., L.D.S., England. Published by the Oxford University Press.

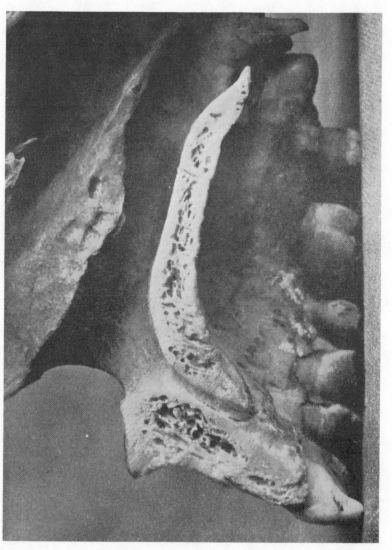

FIGURE 21. HARD PALATE OF THE MOUTH, SHOWING THE DIPLOE

The whole is considerably magnified

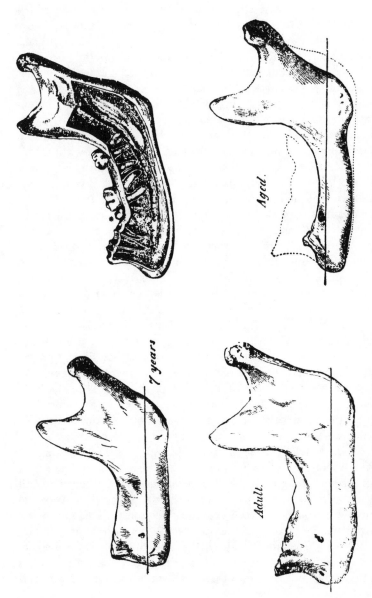

FIGURE 22. JAW BONES, SHOWING SECTIONS OF TRUE BONE AND ALVEOLUS

of light, spongy bone which rests upon the basal portion of the jaw, that is the true bone. The drawings which comprise Figure 22 show the jaw-bone at seven years, at full age, and in old age. The alveolar part of the jaw is that which is above the horizontal line, the true bone is below it. It will be noticed how the alveolar part of the jaw changes. It seems to exist only as a setting for the teeth. It is barely present in old age. From this it will be apparent that there is not such a place as the ' spot where the hard palate meets the teeth.' The teeth are embedded in alveolus, as shown in the upper drawing, and the alveolus is continuous with, that is to say joins, the hard palate. Figure 23 shows an enlargement of a tooth with the surrounding alveolus in which it is set.

There is no doubt that many readers will look upon much of this detail as superfluous and unnecessary, and demand a return to vocal work and not a consideration of dentistry. I would remind such students that ' there are no water-tight compartments in science ' ; and the aim of this volume is to show that the head is a wind instrument, and that consequently vocal tone cannot possibly be produced by the vocal cords. In these dental details we have yet one more link in the chain of evidence. Let the reader turn to Figure 19, and it will be seen that according to the principles here set forth, the vibrating air leaving the sinuses at X, and also slightly to the left of C, would strike directly downwards upon the *top* of the hard palate. Now we have shown that the teeth are set in alveolus, which is continuous with the hard palate ; therefore they will necessarily partake in the vibrations which the hard palate communicates to the air in the mouth. Hence we have an intelligent and satisfying reason for the advice to feel the tone at the teeth, in the place of an unscientific dogma. The division of the jaw into the two sections, bone and alveolus, still further strengthens the theoretical position, for had the teeth been set in bone they would undoubtedly have felt at times so much vibration as to cause extreme discomfort. This is avoided by the spongy texture of the alveolar portion of the jaw. When in old age the teeth fall away, the alveolus having finished its work, gradually disappears. Thus in even the smallest detail has Nature arranged with the utmost solicitude for our comfort and well-being.

From a practical point of view there can be but little difference in the method of a singer's practice, whether sound is produced

FIGURE 23.
TOOTH (RIGHT UPPER MOLAR)
WITH ALVEOLUS (MAGNIFIED)

by the cords themselves or in the space just above them, as stated by Mr. Van Brockhoven ; but there is an enormous difference in the method of practice when the learner ascertains the fact that sound is *made* in the head. The seat or centre of activity is then no longer the throat, but the spot well above the bridge of the nose between the eyes. It is from this spot that the breath is drawn downwards and sound thereby produced. Then at once the whole of the larynx region becomes quiet and placid and a ' throaty ' tone is impossible.

There is in science a principle known as the principle of least action. The workings of the principle are not confined to science, but are also applicable and intensely valuable in art. To the vocalist it is indeed a guiding light, and will help the student out of many a dark corner of difficulty, providing he has learned the correct method of dealing with the subject.

Dr. Latson, an American surgeon, writes : ' Any muscular action of the throat will impair—may absolutely ruin—the tone.'

The pupil must be made to realize that in breathing only, the air movement does not go higher than the nose ; but in singing it has a longer journey to take before it leaves the body, as it continues its course upwards past the nostrils, so into the head, and then returns down the nostrils in a state of vibration, that is to say, as sound, the vibrations having been caused by the tortuous passages through which the breath has travelled, and also by the several slight bony obstructions or pillars past which it has had to go.

Signor Alessandro Bonci, the well-known operatic tenor, says :[1] ' The great secret of voice production is relaxity. Every tone should be produced without an effort, and without any apparent stiffening of the muscles.' This is quite true as far as it goes, but it does not go far enough. There should not only be no ' *apparent* stiffening of the muscles,' but *all* stiffening of any possible kind should be absent. Although Signor Bonci tells us ' the great secret of voice production,' he does not tell us how to make use of that secret. In the theories contained in this book, we learn the important knowledge how physically to proceed in order to obtain ' the great secret of relaxity.' A medical man writing for a London journal in August 1921 gives his readers what he states to be ' one

[1] Extract from ' How to learn to sing,' by Signor Bonci. *Daily Mail*, 30th June 1908.

of the great secrets of Caruso's wonderful voice.' One naturally feels a rush of excitement and enthusiasm when one learns that the price of a daily paper is to put one in possession of such a tremendously valuable ' secret.' Unfortunately the expectations are but short-lived, for we are told ' that it lay in the formation of the epiglottis which was thick at the base . . . but exquisitely fine and delicate at the free end.' The epiglottis is a leaf-shaped cartilage the function of which is to assist in covering over the windpipe when we swallow. (See Figure 1, facing page 11.)

The information concerning Caruso's epiglottis may be interesting, but it would have been quite as useful to the vocalist, and certainly as much to the point, had we been told what size gloves the great tenor wore, or the measurement of his feet.

A critic once asked me : ' Do you, then, maintain that the larynx mechanism cannot produce *any* sound ? ' I replied that I would not like to make such a positive statement. It is quite possible to walk across a room on one's hands only, with the feet in the air ; but this does not prove that such a plan is the correct method of locomotion. It is quite possible to play the piano standing with one's back to it, but the best results are not likely to be produced thereby. So it may be possible for the vocal cords to produce sound ; in fact, by blowing through an excised pair, sound has been produced, but this does not prove that music can be thus generated, or that the larynx is intended by Nature to be the seat of sound. By means of the breath a blade of grass placed between the thumbs can be made to produce a considerable sound ; but no one would regard a blade of grass as a musical instrument.

An argument that may be brought forward in this connection is that in singing and speaking one can often *feel* the vibrations taking place in the upper part of the chest. This is undoubtedly a fact, but Dr. Aikin remarks in his book *The Voice*, 'We have no ground to believe that the solid vibrations of the chest, throat and face are sources of sound, or have any influence outside our own bodies, or we might reasonably expect that the wearing of a comforter or an overcoat would impair the tone of the voice.' Thus only those vibrations that travel directly away from the immediate source of sound can be considered as of any value in tone-production.

Sound of any kind not only travels with the wind, but also against it. One knows that with a favourable wind in a certain direction, the sound of church bells will travel a considerable distance. If there be no wind, the sound will not travel as far in the same direction ; whilst with the wind in the opposite quarter, it will go but a very short way towards the same point of the compass. Let us consider our own singing on exactly the same lines. We regard our head as the seat of sound, and we wish from that centre to allow as many vibrations as possible to travel towards the audience, therefore we should permit the smallest possible number of vibrations to move downwards *against* the flow of the breath (*i.e.*, on to the chest) because these are lost to our hearers in the same way as all the tones of the church bells which travel against the wind are lost to the listener who takes up a position in the direction from which the wind is blowing. We want the tone we produce to travel as far as possible in front of us, therefore, granting that sound is made in the head, the fewer the vibrations which travel to the chest the more there will be to go towards our audience. It is not always possible to prevent some of the tone travelling downwards, because, as we know, sound will travel against the wind, and so it will against the column of air which is travelling upwards, but let the vocalist be careful to control the vibrations as much as possible, so that the very smallest amount is wasted in going in the wrong direction.

Let it be remembered, however, that a comparatively small amount of vibration will produce considerable tonal sensations in the region of the chest and throat, because the muscles here are very sensitive. Let the reader take a tuning fork, and, having struck it, place the vibrating portion against the lips, and it will be noticed how sensitive the nerves are to the movement. If the head of the fork be placed against the finger-nail, no such tenderness will be experienced. So with vocal vibrations. There is no soft tissue in the head (where sound is produced) save the mucous membrane which lines all the sinuses and nasal passages, therefore the same amount of vibration which in the larynx region is easily felt is quite unnoticed in the head.

Further, I would say that one thing is quite certain, viz., that no one who has gone through a course of training on the system which includes the ' shock of the glottis,' ' chest voice,' ' mixed voice,' and other misleading terms, would have any doubt as to which is the better plan, after experiencing the absolute simplicity and the power for improving and strengthening the tone which is the invariable result of vocal work carried out on the principle of head or Sinus Tone Production.

Lecturing upon ' The Borderland of Chemistry and Electricity,' at the Royal Artillery Institution, Woolwich, in November 1898 the late Mr. William Webster, F.C.S., stated : ' Everything in the history of the evolution of the human race points to a better condition of life since science has been applied to the wants of man.' Many and many a person can testify that in all vocality, whether it be the gymnastic display of the opera singer, or the steady, impressive tone of the lecturer, the whole territory of vocalization can be controlled with infinitely greater ease when the science of acoustics, as herein set forth, is applied to it.

We have now arrived at what seems to be a veritable climax. We have considered the possibilities of Sinus Tone Production, and the probabilities of vocal cord tone production. If the matter be considered from an unbiased point of view—perhaps a difficult thing to do, especially when we bear in mind the number of years that vocal cord vibration has been accepted as gospel truth— but if, I repeat, the matter be reasoned out from an unbiased point of view, there can be little doubt as to which system is correct.

Should, however, any one still be undecided, surely the following facts must remove his doubts as easily as a north-east gale can disperse a puff of smoke.

Professor Huxley once said that Herbert Spencer's idea of a tragedy was ' a deduction slain by a fact.'

The following tabulated facts must surely go far to slay the deduction so universally held, that voice is created by the vocal cords. The authority I am about to quote is Dr. Douglas Harmer, M.C. Cantab., F.R.C.S. England, Surgeon to the Throat and Nose Department of St. Bartholomew's Hospital. In writing Section IV of *A System of Operative Surgery*, he says :

I hope it will soon become genuinely recognized that the radical operation of thyrotomy for removal of early intrinsic malignant disease is attended by a remarkable number of complete cures, and compares favourably with almost any other operation for similar conditions in other parts of the body. Butlin, Semon, and C. Jackson, have all obtained in recent years from sixty to eighty per cent. of lasting cures. . . . The condition of the patient after thyrotomy—The voice results are often surprisingly good, even when free excision of soft parts, including one or both of the vocal cords, has been required. In from forty to sixty per cent. of cases that are cured the voice is *practically normal*,[1] though rough and reduced in volume and range. Of the remainder, the majority recover sufficiently to produce a considerable whisper, and only a few suffer complete loss of voice. The causes of a complete loss of voice, when it occurs, are chronic inflammation, cicatricial contractions,[2] or improper union of the cartilage.

Let us consider now the full meaning of this. If the eyes of a man be taken out, can he see ? If the ears of a man be taken away, can he hear ? Doubtless there can only be one answer to these questions. Yet we have it on the highest authority that when the vocal cords of a man are cut out he can still speak, and the voice remains ' practically normal.' The only alteration which takes place is one that quite agrees with the tenets of Sinus Tone Production, viz. : the voice is reduced in volume and range. The ' breath-governors ' being absent, there is naturally less control in directing the air column from one sinus to another.

But, if the vocal cords are the seat of sound, *nothing short of a miracle* could at all explain the continuance of the power of speech after their excision.

This, however, does not exhaust the contradictions, and, we may add, the absurdities of the vocal cord theories of sound production.

Dr. Harmer continues :

The voice after laryngectomy.[3]——In some cases . . . a whispered voice remains, even after the pharynx has been completely shut off from the air passages, and as shown by experience, may be developed by practice until it is quite sufficient for the demands of the patient. Hans Schmidt's case has become more or less celebrated, in which under conditions of this sort, a loud, though rough and monotonous voice was developed. One of Mikulicz's patients was even able to sing.

Le Bulletin Médical of Paris for 17th April 1887 contains most interesting reading upon the same matter. Dr. Gougenheim writes of a man whose true vocal cords had been eradicated in consequence of disease. The epiglottis of this patient had been destroyed by ulcerations ; his voice, though husky, eventually became sonorous, and he could sing a scale.

Dr. Moura introduces a patient who, having undergone the complete removal of the larynx, could make himself heard.

Dr. Fauvel mentions a case where the whole larynx had been

---

[1] The italics are mine.

[2] Cicatricial contractions are the contractions made by a wound after an operation, should it heal unevenly. See Glossary.

[3] Laryngectomy is the cutting away of the whole of the larynx.

G

taken right away by Dr. Péan fourteen months previously on account of an epithelioma. This epithelioma had been diagnosed by Dr. Poyet and verified at the laboratory of M. Cornil. Notwithstanding his loss, the patient's voice was loud enough to make his conversation heard at a distance of several yards.

Record of another interesting case comes from Vienna, where, in 1859, Professor Joh. Czermak read before the Academy of Sciences an account of one of his patients whose vocal cords had joined together through ulceration, thus completely closing the air-passage. Breathing was carried on by means of a little tube inserted in the windpipe below the cords, and the patient was able to speak.

Yet another instance must be given, and that a very important one, because it occurred in my own practice. A medical man introduced to me one of his patients, a man about 28 years of age, who for 25 years had been unable to speak clearly, in consequence of the destruction of *both* vocal cords by a corrosive acid. This man was sent to me as a kind of test case. What was the result ?

In two months he was able to speak clearly, and to sing a simple melody ; and although the tone of his voice was not altogether beautiful, yet it was certainly not objectionable, and he had the compass of an octave under excellent control.[1]

Several medical men expressed the opinion that I had merely taught the man to use his false vocal cords, in place of the real ones. Such a statement might well be regarded as amusing, were it not for the serious side of the question, which shows how unwilling some men are to accept progress unless it dovetails with their preconceived ideas.

In the first place, the man was quite unaware that he possessed false vocal cords. He had never even heard of them ; so it was hardly likely he would be able to control them as stated.

Secondly : If the medical profession knows of some method whereby the false vocal cords can be persuaded to act in place of the true, why has not that method been made public, and why had not the system been used by doctors on the man ?

Thirdly and chiefly : Any elementary schoolboy knows that tone cannot be produced from a cord which is *curved* and unstrained. The shape and condition of the false vocal cords

[1] See *Light on the Voice Beautiful*, page 170. Published by James Clarke.

may be represented thus ⌒⌒, see Figure 28, facing page 115, and we repeat, any child knows that such a cord cannot possibly produce tone.

When Dame Nature departs from her beaten track and takes an unusual course, then is the opportunity for her admirers to discover something new as to her plans and laws, 'for it has been found,' wrote Dr. Harvey, 'in almost all things, that what they contain of useful or of applicable is hardly perceived unless we are deprived of them, or they become deranged in some way.'

It was disease of the thyroid gland which taught us what the healthy thyroid gland really does for us. In similar manner it was ' derangement' of the vocal cords which first led me to realize how utterly unsound and contradictory were the many creeds which were—and still are—held concerning them. Then followed the serious and very complicated problem of ascertaining the true position they should hold, and consequently, the exact work they were intended to perform in Nature's system.

We are continually making use of our voices, and in doing so we can feel the vocal cords vibrate, and, with the laryngoscope, we can also see them move. Moreover, our throats are usually sore if we lose our voice. This is considered proof positive that the vocal cords create tone, and no amount of merely theoretical argument will convince some people to the contrary.

There are also many who regard the mere fact that the doctrine of vocal cord sonority is universally accepted as sufficient evidence of its soundness.

When, however, the wonderful skill of Sir Henry Butlin, Sir Felix Semon, Dr. Pean, and others has shown us that the vocal cords may be taken right away and the patient's voice remains ' practically normal' surely it is time to give up a theory which is so evidently impossible, and, one might add, even ridiculous.

Another point, too, is worth consideration. Had these patients received instruction in the proper method of Sinus Tone Production, it is only reasonable to suppose that the ' roughness' of their voices could have been lessened, and the compass somewhat increased.

May we not see in all these facts and details an endorsement of the proverb uttered by the wise king : ' It is the glory of God to conceal a matter' (Prov. xxv, 2) ?

It is, however, a jealous world, and the apostles of the present—
as a body—have no love for those who show the weak spots
of favourite doctrines, and boldly proclaim a newer and a
better way. ' It is even more immoral for a man to be too
far in front than to be too far behind,' says Samuel Butler ;
and history has long proclaimed the same with no uncertain
voice. One reason is probably because ' no body of men cares
to have it shown that their good will is more notable than their
good sense.' Harvey was a ' crack-brain,' Beethoven was ' mad,'
Whistler was a ' coxcomb ' ; and even the scientist, Sir William
Ramsay, ' like most discoverers, did not escape the flail of
severe criticism.'[1]

And what shall be said of the man who dares to dethrone the
vocal cords from the kingdom of song ?

It must be owned that there have not been wanting those who
have hurled against him their ' shafts of bitter satire.' But this is
no wonder. The average man—and the world is peopled chiefly
by the ' average ' person—strongly objects to be disturbed and
made uncomfortable in his armchair of tenets which, notwithstanding some awkward excrescences, has supported him all his
life. He is angry at any interference with his ease and comfort,
and prefers to be left alone.

' Great is Diana of the Ephesians,' cried the silver craftsmen of
old, and their indignation knew no bounds as they realized that
the honour of their goddess was at stake, and that their special
trade was in danger.

But, if Diana be a false goddess, she must fall, notwithstanding
all the power and enthusiasm of her adherents. Her beauty and
her antiquity can avail her nothing against the stern, strong power
of truth.

How many Dianas have fallen since those early days of Christianity ! How many men have endured hard words, cruel sarcasm,
and sometimes death itself, in order that they might raise either
the knowledge or some system of the world to a higher level and
a truer basis, so that their brethren might benefit thereby !

But it has been said : ' The only price that can be paid for
genius is suffering, and this is the only wages it can receive.' Why
should this be so ? The reason is that a man is not usually willing

[1] Extract from Sir William Crookes's Presidential Address before the
British Association for the Advancement of Science, 1898.

to acknowledge that he is in any way inferior to his neighbour. Still, I can say truly with Horace Greeley, ' I do not regret having braved public opinion when I knew it was wrong, and was quite sure it would be merciless.'

The novelist Thackeray was one day seen looking at a grocer's window wherein were two bags of sugar, one marked 10½d. and the other 11d. As he left the window he was heard to say, ' How they must hate each other ! '

We may be thankful there is another side to human nature, and I hasten to acknowledge my indebtedness to it. I have received generous encouragement and kindness from some people who have taken an interest in my work. Needless to say, I am hoping that I may find still more friends—artistic friends, scientific friends, and, perhaps, even personal friends—who will help in proclaiming the undoubted fact that vocalization is getting free from the bonds of mere imitation, which have so long fettered it, and is becoming in its own right a healthy, vigorous, and definite science.

CHAPTER IV

THE VOCAL MECHANISM OF THE LOWER ANIMALS

May the realities of life dispel for you its illusions.—RICHTER.

DOCTOR William Harvey, in trying to convince his too conservative brethren as to the excellence and value of his discoveries in relation to the heart and its functions, expressed himself as follows :

. . . Since, therefore, from the foregoing considerations, and many others to the same effect, it is plain that what has heretofore been said concerning the motions and functions of the heart and arteries must appear obscure or inconsistent, or even impossible, to him who carefully considers the entire subject ; it will be proper to look more narrowly into the matter ; to contemplate the motion of the heart and arteries not only in man, but in all animals that have hearts ; and further, by . . . constant ocular inspection to investigate and endeavour to find the truth.

If the reader will kindly read the above extract again, and in doing so substitute the words ' *vocal cords* ' for ' heart and arteries,' a correct idea will probably then be formed as to the contents of this chapter.

Let us, then, follow Dr. William Harvey's example, and study and compare the anatomy—so far as it concerns us—of different families in the animal world.

The first detail to note is that in the case of such animals as the cow, sheep, dog, etc., each has sinuses in some form. There is naturally a considerable difference in shape and other details : *e.g.*, the frontal sinus of the ox is prolonged into the core of its horns, but it has no sphenoid sinus. In place of this there are irregular cavities in the hard palate of the mouth which communicate with the maxillary sinus on each side. The turbinated bones of the dog and the cat are particularly distinguished for numerous convolutions, instead of continuing in a straight line, as in the human head. Special peculiarities in other animals could be mentioned, but these will answer the purpose. Now, if the reader will take particular note of the quality of tone produced by a cow in calling, it will be quite clear that such a tone is not likely to be produced by vocal cord vibration. It is quite as unlike string vibration as the tone of a cornet is to the string tone of a violin. The sound is undoubtedly due to air vibration in a hard, hollow chamber. A similar timbre can be observed in the neigh of a horse, or the bay of a big watch-dog. Beyond this, anyone who has the power of locating sound would certainly detect that the sound made by a cow does not emanate from the throat, neither has it a ' throaty ' quality. Even the common or garden cat may teach us a lesson. Let the reader imagine a cat's catastrophic cataclysm of caterwauling ca(t)cophany, which, being interpreted, means a quarrel between two or more pussies. When they stand eyeing each other, with lashing tails, number one will start a sound on quite a high pitch, which will gradually descend the scale. Number two will follow on in exactly the same way, the high note gradually falling to a low one. Now it must be quite evident that these two angry creatures are not singing to each other ; their mentality is engaged in a quarrel, as is seen in the subsequent fight. The descending scale can only be explained in this way. The cat takes a full breath, and the air passing through the head at high pressure produces a high note ; as the lungs get empty the pressure naturally decreases and the tone falls, following exactly the same laws as wind through a keyhole, namely, the greater the pressure, the higher is the pitch of the note. Thus we get another example of the first postulate of science in the uniformity of Nature. Had the sound been produced by varying tension of the vocal cords, we should be obliged to consider that the animals had some musical intentions, in which case a low note might well precede a high note, whereas the reverse is always the case. Surely, then, if these quadrupeds produce sounds by air vibrations in the head, it seems highly improbable that human beings with vocal cords and sinuses of a somewhat similar construction should work on a totally different principle.

Birds, too, although not possessing any large sinuses, yet on the whole are more abundantly supplied with air in the skull than any other vertebrates. The bony structure of the head consists of an outer and an inner wall, connected with a beautifully delicate filigree work, also of bone, so that the whole skull is permeated with air. An important lesson which many singing masters and students might learn from the birds is the fact that they invariably devote some time to *piano* or muted practice before they begin to use their full voice.

From a bird to an elephant is rather a big leap, but a lesson may be learned from each. The trumpet of an elephant can be heard at the distance of a mile. Can we imagine any string-produced tone carrying so far as this ? An elephant has enormous sinuses, and it is not difficult to realize that by this means his voice would be heard far and near.

A point of very considerable interest is the fact that snakes have no head sinuses, and it is well known that the only sound a snake makes is a hiss.[1] This surely may be looked upon as a link in the chain of evidence. It was a certain kind of hiss, that is to say, an *escape* of breath, that I noticed in the patient mentioned on page 15 ; now that she consciously directs her breath through the sinuses, there is no sound of air escape whatever.

We know, however, that a theory which has been accepted as gospel truth for hundreds of years will not die without a struggle. The first medical man to give vocal cords the value which they hold to-day was the famous Greek physician and anatomist, Galen[2] (A.D. 130 to 200), court physician to the Roman Emperor, Marcus Aurelius. Before his day it was thought that the voice proceeded from the heart. It was, therefore, at his suggestion, and based on his authority that the larynx has for the last 1700 years been universally recognized as the seat of sound ; and doubtless, there are many who will consider it absolutely impious to question such ancient and catholic tenets.

Indeed, when one calls to mind such names as Vesalius, the 'Father of Anatomy' ; M. Flourens, the distinguished French physiologist ; the late Sir Henry Butlin, Sir J. Milsom Rees, Mr. Cyril Horsford, and many other eminent present-day throat specialists, it is not without some show of reason that a charge of impertinence may perhaps be laid against me.

Possibly the chief reason that medical men have failed to see the weakness and the contradictions of the vocal cord theory is the fact that the department of the science of acoustics which relates to the laws of sound has not been included in the scheme of their education. The cause of the omission is obvious. At the outset of his career the medical student is faced with such an array of subjects which he has to master during his years of apprenticeship

---

[1] Rattlesnakes of course make a rattle, but the material for this sound is in the tail, and consists of a number of loose, horny rings, or bell-like structures, which fit into one another.

[2] Appendix G, page 166.

that any additional burden must be added only under the plea of urgent necessity, lest it should prove like the final straw upon the back of the proverbial camel. Latin, chemistry, anatomy, surgery, hygiene—to say nothing of legal and many other details, form a curriculum which may well keep the average man in full study and employment.

On the other hand, the music student has an equally trying ordeal to face. Many hours every week must be spent in the practice of harmony and counterpoint, much time in the endeavour to master at least one musical instrument, while a passing acquaintance must be made with two or three others. The history of music will certainly demand attention, also the very necessary 'art of teaching.' One or two foreign languages must be added, besides a more or less intimate knowledge of music itself, both British and foreign. Occasionally the study of acoustics is included, with a smattering of jargon about vocal cords, gleaned from a book by some more or less competent writer. Is it, then, a matter for surprise to find that the music student has had no more opportunity for the real *study* of anatomy, surgery, and acoustics, than the medical student has found for the *study* of the science of music ?

Beyond that, the necessity for such a combination has not apparently occurred to any of our tutorial dons.

In the *Daily Telegraph* for Thursday 20th January 1916 an interesting article appeared by Dr. William Garnett, entitled ' British Trade and Applied Science.' In it he states : ' The habit of living, working and thinking in compartments is too apparent throughout our educational system.' On 24th January a letter appeared in the same journal over the signature, ' Frederick Davis,' wherein a similar thought was expressed, viz. : ' There are no water-tight compartments in science.'

The work of the present author has been to break down the massive partitions which have hitherto divided anatomy, acoustics, and singing, and by so doing to open up for the human voice a long vista of possibilities, which were previously regarded as impossible.

Now, just as ' Galileo and William Harvey refused to be bound by the teachings of Aristotle and Galen, and appealed from these authorities to the actual facts of Nature,' so, ' by putting on one side authority, and directly appealing to observation and experiment,'[1] have I endeavoured to show a more reasonable and more practical method of vocal control and development than can generally be attained by the system of vocal cord tone production.

Unquestionably, the ideas herein set forth are full of iconoclasm, and I feel much sympathy with William Harvey, who, in sending forth his own revolutionary book in 1628, wrote : ' What remains to be said . . . is of so novel and unheard of character, that I not only fear injury to myself from the envy of a few, but I tremble lest I have mankind at large for my enemies, so much doth wont and custom . . . and respect for antiquity influence all men.'

There are, of course, those who will not admit anything, unless it be upon what they consider high authority. To such this volume will have but very little interest. It appeals only to those who are willing to investigate and endeavour to find the truth ; ' for true philosophers,' wrote the same William Harvey more than 300 years ago, ' who are only eager for truth and knowledge, never regard themselves as already so thoroughly informed, but that they welcome further information from whomsoever and from whencesoever it may come ; nor are they so narrow-minded as to imagine any of the arts or sciences transmitted to us by the ancients, in such a state of forwardness or completeness that nothing is left for the ingenuity or industry of others.'

Let us now pursue the study of the animal creation a little further. Lord Lister found valuable information in the study of frogs, but we will turn to the sheep, and we find that in the larynx of the sheep the vocal cords do not project beyond the general surface. They are practically flush with the surrounding tissue. The texture of the cords also gives the impression that they do not possess much elasticity, and it is quite certain that they do not present any sharp edge, as exists in the human larynx, and also in the case of monkeys.[2]

This gives us two undoubted facts, which no amount of argument or mere opinion can alter.

There is the snake, without any sinus. This creature cannot make any sound beyond the hiss. There is the sheep, practically

[1] Editor's Introduction to Harvey's *Circulation of the Blood*. Published by J. M. Dent & Sons Ltd. in Everyman's Library.

[2] It is interesting to note the sphenoid sinuses in sheep are practically non-existent.

without vocal cords, but with sinuses, and this animal can call and make itself understood amongst its fellows.

How can these facts be accounted for, if the vocal cords create tone ?

We now turn to another point of interest, viz., the silence of the giraffe. Realizing that such a peculiarity must of necessity have a physical cause, I determined to ascertain, if possible, the physical cause of the animal being dumb. It must be confessed that the unravelling of the question caused me considerable anxiety, because, at one time, it seemed to show that my theories were untenable ; but the reason for this was, that I had not pursued the matter to its proper conclusion. How many times the earnest student and searcher for truth has been brought suddenly to a standstill, face to face with facts which apparently overthrew the whole system he had been so long and carefully elaborating ! The first step was to ascertain if the giraffe has vocal cords, and what position they occupy in his long neck. So far as I could ascertain, the question had not previously occurred to anyone ; but I eventually found that, practically speaking, the animal does not possess vocal cords. In the position where one would expect to find these cords is a certain amount of tissue which stands in their place, but this is flush with the surrounding surface, as in the case of the sheep, and therefore, of no practical value in sound-production. It was evident that this discovery would not help forward my theories. I hoped however, to find that the animal was also without sinuses, but was disappointed at finding that it was plentifully endowed with these cavities. Thus, my researches seemed to give the very opposite results to those for which I had hoped. This was intensely disappointing to me ; but feeling certain that further work would reveal details which I had not yet grasped, I determined to continue my studies, and eventually succeeded, to my great joy, in getting to the root of the matter.

If the reader will now turn forward to Figures 24 and 25 we will endeavour to make clear the various points which bear upon our subject. Figure 24 shows a skull cut in halves from back to front, that is to say, from between the horns to the tip of the nose. In that half of the skull which is undermost, a series of large sinuses can be seen between the points A and A_3. In Figure 25 the same sinuses can be seen from another point of view, that is, from a position behind the head. Here they are shown in four sections cut crosswise, that is, from one side of the head to the other. The two which claim our attention are marked respectively E and B. The points A_1 and A_2 in Figure 25 correspond to the points A_1 and A_2 in Figure 24. Section B, Figure 25, is a continuation towards the nose of section C. In the same sections the animal's teeth are seen at $G\ G$. The cavity at J holds the brain. In section B, directly above the arch of the mouth, is the nasal passage. If the reader will look at the points indicated by $H\ H\ H\ H$ and join them by four imaginary lines, a rough square will be obtained which will denote the extent of the nose without the sinuses, Surrounding the nasal passage, above and on either side, are the sinuses A_1, A_4, and A_5. The position of sinuses A_4 and A_5 in Figure 25 cannot be shown in Figure 24. The sinuses at A_4 on the left side of section B, Figure 25, are not quite as distinct as those at A_5 on the right side ; but it will be readily understood that the two sides are similar in construction.

Closely fitting into each nostril are three elongated hollow cones of bony net-work of most beautiful and delicate structure, which fit closely together and partly overlap. Figure 26 is a photograph of one of them. They can also be seen in their natural positions, as indicated by the letters L_1 and $L,\ L$ in Figures 24 and 25. That half of the skull which is uppermost in Figure 24 gives the clearest idea of them. These in the giraffe are the turbinated bones, corresponding to those in the human head described on pages 17 and 47. It will, however, be noticed that there is but little similarity between the two kinds.

Having endeavoured to explain, as far as necessary, the anatomy of the head, let us see what lesson we can learn from it, so that we may ascertain what is the cause of the animal being dumb.

The absence of vocal cords cannot give a satisfactory reason, because the cords of a sheep are almost identical with those of the giraffe, and we know that the sheep can speak clearly to those of its own kind.

The explanation is found in the fact that the entrance to the sinuses of the giraffe is at the *floor* of the nose at the point indicated by K in Figure 25, and just about the position of L in Figure 24, and then the passages run upwards and backwards towards the point marked A_3. In this figure the entrance itself cannot be shown because it is the *other side* of the turbinated bones. As a

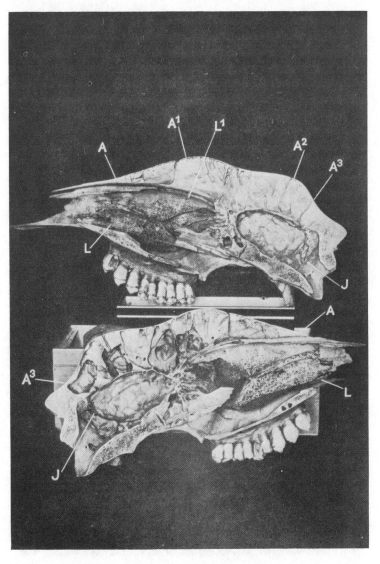

FIGURE 24. SKULL OF GIRAFFE (SIDE SECTION)
An explanation of the Key letters appears on pages 91, 92 and 93.

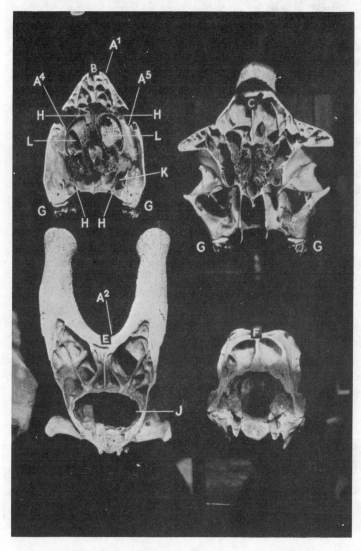

FIGURE 25. SKULL OF GIRAFFE (CROSS SECTION)
An explanation of the Key letters appears on pages 91 and 92.

FIGURE 26. TURBINATED BONE OF A GIRAFFE

matter of fact, the finding of this entrance caused me considerable trouble, so well is it protected.

Now it will be obvious that the outcoming breath, having travelled from the lungs to the point indicated L in Figure 24, could not possibly be compelled at that point to travel backwards and upwards towards A_3. The incoming air is also powerless to make a sound because it can only get to the sinuses by first *percolating* through the network of turbinated bones. A column of air would necessarily be broken up in passing through them. Thus the very same part of anatomy which in man can by skill be made to assist vocalization, in the case of the giraffe acts as a preventive.

Let us now consider and sum up the contents of this chapter.

We find the snake, without sinuses, unable to make any sound beyond a hiss. The giraffe, without vocal cords, but with sinuses, over which it can exercise no control, also dumb. The sheep, without vocal cords and with sinuses, able to speak well—to its own kind. The tone-quality of the voice in the cow, the horse, and the dog demands attention, likewise the power of the elephant's voice. In weighing up these various facts, it surely must be admitted that we have a considerable amount of interesting information, which goes far to endorse the theories set forth in this volume.

How soon the idea of Sinus Tone Production will be generally accepted and carried out time alone will show, but no one can prove that the theories are unscientific or impossible.

It must be admitted that there have not been wanting both musical and medical men who have thought it right to point the finger of scorn at the whole scheme. They have, moreover, conclusively proved, to their own entire satisfaction, that the whole system of Sinus Tone Production is a fallacy. It is however, important to know that these same people have never put the theories to any really practical test. ' By what reasoning,' wrote Dr. William Harvey, ' should we give the blind from birth to know that the sun was luminous and far surpassed the stars in brightness ? Who would pretend to persuade those who had never tasted wine that it was a drink much pleasanter to the palate than water ? '

The arguments which for 300 years had been accepted as true with respect to the circulation of the blood, are not less correct when applied to the two systems of tone production now under consideration. The only statement that can be truly brought against my system is that, according to present notions, it is heretical.

Still, any student knows that what stands as truth in one generation is often found to be false in the next. The *Daily Telegraph*, in its issue of 9th June 1914, very aptly says : ' " Absurd ! " may be the verdict of to-day, but the absurdities of one age are the commonplaces of the next.' So I am convinced that before many years have passed it will be seen and realized—to the great benefit of the human race—that the vocal cords are not, and cannot be, sound producers. Let it not be thought that the case is overstated in declaring that it will be to the ' great benefit of the human race.' Previous to 1909 when *Science and Singing* was first published, there had not been any book either musical or medical which gave systematic and controllable value to the sinuses. The frontal sinuses were unused excepting indeed by Jenny Lind, Sims Reeves, and artists of this stamp, who unknowingly owed their voice to their ability to use the frontal sinuses. When unused they naturally get clogged with mucus which, being unable to escape, eventually becomes putrescent and breeds disease, not infrequently consumption. Many and many a person who has learned to clear his head of what has become filthy and decomposed matter, can testify to renewed health, freedom from headache and a return of healthy colour to the cheeks through the simple but essential work of keeping the sinuses in a healthy condition.

On the principles enunciated in this work, deafness can be— and has been—relieved, and the most confirmed cases of stammering can be cured. Men who have stuttered from early childhood have been shown, much to their own joy, how their speech may flow easily and freely.

Further, I am quite convinced that, by continued thought and work on these lines, it will be possible to reduce considerably the number of those people who are deaf and dumb, and the affliction may become almost a thing of the past.

The sinuses have hitherto been looked upon merely as a means of making the osseous portion of the cranium light in structure. It has been considered that their only office was a negative one, viz., the avoidance of weight. The question of their possibilities as a sound-producing instrument opens up a new and wide field for investigation. For the scientific man with time at his disposal, there are many interesting experiments to conduct which might be very fruitful in yielding important practical results to the medical and also to the musical world.

Should these experiments eventually prove that it is impossible to cure the deaf and dumb by means of Sinus Tone Production, there will still remain the fact that the system is of incalculable benefit to all who have the power of speech and song. This is a fact which can be testified to by many persons who have previously been considerable sufferers from throat troubles. Should time show that too much has been claimed for the work, in expecting it to release the dumb from their affliction, even then the limitation will only be an endorsement of the sentiment written by Goethe, ' Man errs as long as he is striving.' and there will yet be the comforting thought, so well expressed by the late Sir Hubert Parry in his book, *The Art of Music*: ' Though men may be deceived in hoping too much and attempting the impossible, progress would be even slower than it is if no one were capable of heroic mistakes.' A great experimental philosopher is reported to have said, ' Show me the scientific man who never made a mistake, and I will show you one who never made a discovery.' For ' in every department of thought advance is only made when men will make experiments and put forward suggestions, some of which, after due consideration, may win their way to acceptance, while others will be rejected.'[1] Prof. J. A. Thomson expresses the same idea in the following interesting manner. He says : ' The scientific imagination devises a possible solution to a difficulty, and the investigator proceeds to test it. He makes intellectual keys and then tries whether they fit the lock. If the hypothesis does not fit, it is rejected, and another is made. The scientific workshop is full of discarded keys.'

The very existence of this present volume is a proof that Sinus Tone Production is by no means a 'discarded key,' but is winning its ' way to acceptance.' Further and independent testimony can be found in the August 1913 issue of the American magazine, *The Musician*, where Dr. Herbert Sanders speaks of the theory as ' a belief which is gaining ground.'

Besides these open and visible proofs, there is yet another,

[1] From Rev. H. B. Streeter's Introduction to *Foundations*, by Seven Oxford Men. Published by the Macmillan Co.

which is not less certain, although less obvious. This is the fact
that a very large number of tutors are more or less vaguely adopting
the method. Although it is usually recognized that ' imitation is
the sincerest form of flattery,' yet in this case it must be owned
that imitation is anything but a compliment to the original method.

It is true the imitators may produce results which are vastly
better than a whole-hearted and energetic course of vocal cord
treatment, but they can only be regarded as a mere counterfeit of
those which can be obtained by conscientiously and scrupulously
following the tenets of the new belief, even to its smallest detail.

The full importance of some of these apparently trifling details
can only be realized by those who have patiently given time and
thought to the subject. Robert Browning beautifully expresses
the value of these ' littles ' when he says :

> Oh, the little more and how much it is,
> And the little less and what worlds away.

So it is when considering the balance of tone which can be produced by a perfect blend of the four positions of the head sinuses.

CHAPTER V

NERVES

There is no rule or catechism or precedent that is a good
substitute for thinking.—*New York World*.

THE FIRST edition of this work (*Science and Singing*, published
in 1909) had no reference to nerve work. The second edition,
produced in 1918 under the title *The Voice Beautiful in Speech
and Song*, introduced the matter on the understanding that
although 'intensely interesting,' yet it was 'not of vast practical
value.' Since then, continued study and thought, together with
unwearied application, have revealed a truth which in the beginning I little suspected, and which has been a cause of astonishment
both to me and to those who have studied with me. The truth
which has come to light is, that nerve, or (as I prefer to call it)
electric power, is really the simple and marvellously effective
solvent of the numerous difficulties which bar the way to perfect
voice control. Thus it will be seen how exceedingly apt is the
following statement of Sir Joseph Larmor, quoted on page 76 of
the second edition of this work.

In addressing the London Mathematical Society on 13th March
1884 he said : ' It is a matter of constant observation that different
departments of mathematical physics are closely connected
together, so that the solution of a question in one branch of the
subject admits of being transferred into another branch and serving
as the solution of a corresponding problem there.'

It is true we are not here considering mathematical physics, but
we are considering a branch of science which has a mathematical
foundation ; and the quotation is appropriate because hitherto the
study of nerves has had in our minds but little connection with
the art of singing. I can quite realize that many good and artistic
people will strongly disapprove of having another subject introduced for study into the singing world. It must, of course, be
conceded that our excellent vocalists of the past gave no attention
to such matters, but that is no proof that the knowledge of Nature's
system of work is outside the radius of our consideration ; on
the contrary, it constitutes an important link in the present chain

H   97

of argument and theory ; it gives a reasonable and satisfying solution to a difficult acoustic problem ; and, above all, it gives the student a definite and exact control over the voice which, without exaggeration, must be termed wonderful. Let us then consider, so far as it concerns our purpose, the position and work of some of the nerves.

The cranial nerves of the human body are divided by the medical profession, for the purpose of study and classification, into twelve pairs. Fortunately, we are for the present purpose concerned with only three of these sets, viz., the tenth which is known as the vagus nerve, the eleventh which is known as the accessory nerve, and the twelfth, or hypoglossal nerve.

Before considering their functions it will be well to explain that the nerves of our body are divided into three families, viz., sensory, motor, and autonomic nerves.

The autonomic nervous system has a pharyngeal branch which assists in supplying the muscles and the mucous membrane of the pharynx. This however, has no practical bearing on our subject. We may, therefore, dismiss it.

The sensory nerves convey to the brain the senses of touch, of pain, of heat, and of cold.

The motor nerves concern us most at the moment, because it is by the stimuli which they convey to the muscles that we are able to move and also to maintain bodily equilibrium. The nerves terminate in the muscles and are able thus to carry out their work. The muscles separated from the nerves are as useless as a steam engine without steam.

The vagus nerve arises from the brain and takes the longest course over the body of all the cerebral nerves. The two branches of this nerve with which we are most concerned are the superior laryngeal, and the inferior or recurrent laryngeal.

The superior laryngeal nerve is itself divided into two branches, namely, the external branch, which has motor influence, and the internal branch, which is sensory.

The motor influence of the external branch gives control to the crico-thyroid muscles (see explanation of Figure 20). The work of these muscles is to draw the thyroid cartilage downwards, in the direction shown by the arrow, that is to say, towards the cricoid cartilage, on which it hinges. These crico-thyroid muscles are the only muscles controlled by the external branch of the superior laryngeal nerve.

The internal branch of the same nerve is the sensory nerve of the larynx above the vocal cords.

We will now turn to the other branch of the vagus nerve which we are considering, viz., the inferior or recurrent laryngeal nerve. This also has both sensory and motor influence. It conveys sensibility to the larynx below the vocal cords and to the whole of the trachea.[1]

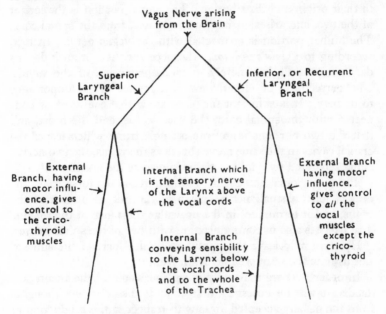

Vagus Nerve arising from the Brain

Superior Laryngeal Branch

Inferior, or Recurrent Laryngeal Branch

External Branch, having motor influence, gives control to the crico-thyroid muscles

Internal Branch which is the sensory nerve of the Larynx above the vocal cords

Internal Branch conveying sensibility to the Larynx below the vocal cords and to the whole of the Trachea

External Branch having motor influence, gives control to all the vocal muscles except the crico-thyroid

BRANCHES OF THE VAGUS NERVE

There are other branches but they need not be considered here.

The motor nerves of this branch control all the muscles of the larynx except the crico-thyroid, which, as already stated, are controlled by the external branch of the superior laryngeal nerve.

For the sake of completeness, we give a diagram showing those muscles which are controlled by the inferior (that is, the recurrent) laryngeal nerve. The above chart will help the reader to understand the divisions of the nerve.

[1] See Figure 1, facing page 11.

We have already said that the vagus nerve has the longest course of all the cerebral nerves. How varied its duties are will be seen when we state that beside its work in the larynx, which has just been explained, it is also connected either directly or indirectly with the heart, lungs, oesophagus, ears, tongue, liver, and other organs.

We now turn to the eleventh, or accessory nerve. This is a purely motor nerve and consists of two parts termed respectively bulbar or accessory, and spinal. They differ from each other both in their origin and distribution. The spinal portion is the longer of the two, and arises, as its name indicates, from the spinal cord. The bulbar portion is connected with the vagus nerve. In fact, according to *Quain's Anatomy* the accessory is not an independent nerve at all, but merely ' a caudal extension of the vagus.' The correctness of either view is a matter of no importance to us here. It is sufficient for us to know that the nerve is connected with the spinal cord, the vocal cords, and the heart, and that the two portions unite into a single trunk which leaves the cranial cavity in the same nerve sheath as the vagus, the two nerves being separated by a fold of tissue known as the arachnoid.[1]

The hypoglossal nerve is the motor nerve to the tongue. In the neck it joins a small nerve known as the lingual branch of the vagus, and it terminates in the muscular substance of the tongue. The nerve is also in communication with two of the spinal nerves.

Here we may leave the purely anatomical part of the subject. Let us now see what we may learn from it.

In order that we may fully grasp the whole of the theoretical details, it will be necessary first of all to dissociate our thoughts from the usually accepted ideas with respect to the production of voice, and to start with a mind free from any bias.

Having accomplished this, doubtless with some difficulty, the first fact we have to grasp is that our sinuses *cannot* be resonators. Let us carefully see how this conclusion can be proved to demonstration.

We must realize at the start that a resonator is a substance or material which increases tone or sound originated by some other material.

It might perhaps appear unnecessary to mention such an apparently elementary truth, but experience has shown how easy

[1] See Appendix H, page 167.

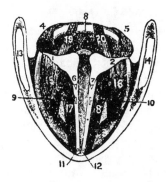

FIGURE 27.[1] VIEW OF A SECTION OF THE LARYNX FROM ABOVE

1–6 and 7–2 are the arytenoid cartilages, as seen at *D D* in Figure 20.

6 and 7 indicate the vocal processes of these cartilages, to which one end of the vocal cords is attached. The other end of the cords is attached to the thyroid cartilage at the points 11–12. Compare with *E* and *C*1 in Figure 20.

From 6 to 11 and from 7 to 12 give the length of the vocal cords.

13 and 14 show the position of the thyroid cartilages which enclose the mechanism of the larynx. Side 14 is identical with· *C C C*1 *C*2 in Figure 20.

The line by the figure 8 shows where the muscle known as the arytenoideus transversus is situated. The function of this muscle is to draw the two arytenoids closer to each other.

The muscles shown at 4–1 and 5–2 (posterior crico-arytenoidei) draw the vocal cords apart, whilst the two pairs at 15–16 (lateral crico-arytenoidei) and 17–18 (thyro-arytenoidei) draw the cords together.

There are many other details which could be mentioned in this Figure, but our purpose is sufficiently served by describing the above.

[1] Taken by permission from *Voice, Song and Speech*, by Lennox Browne, F.R.C.S. Edin., and Emil Behnke. Published by Sampson Low, Marston Co., London.

it is to fall into error. For example, in the chapter on ' Speech '
in Halliburton's *Handbook of Physiology* it is stated : ' When
the larynx is passive and the resonating cavities alone come into
play, then we get whispering.' Here we have a clever and accomplished author, taking away what he believes to be the seat of
sound, viz., the larynx, and making what he believes to be merely
resonating chambers actually produce sound. It would be just as
reasonable to say : ' When you want to get a *pianissimo* on the
violin, let the strings be passive and use the woodwork—that is,
the resonating chamber—only.' As a matter of real fact, Dr. Halliburton's dictum is in my opinion very near to the truth, but
then the sinuses which he calls, and are usually looked upon as,
' resonating cavities,' have a different office to perform on the lines
of sinus tone production, and are considered as the seat of the
creation of tone, not merely its enlargement. Hence the attitude
in the matter herein adopted is a reasonable one, whilst Dr. Halliburton's appears to be the reverse, for he turns what he believes
to be merely resonating cavities into actual sound producers,
without having given us any source from which the sound is produced, ' which is absurd.'

Further it must be obvious to any thinking person, that in
order to serve its purpose, a resonator must be in contact with
that which creates the tone. The vibrations of the violin strings
are communicated to the body of the instrument by means of the
bridge. Separate the strings from the woodwork by ever so tiny
a distance, and there will be no possibility of the wood acting as a
resonator. The strings of the pianoforte are strained across the
bridge which is glued on to the belly—that is, the sounding board
—of the instrument. Surely then, it is only reasonable to suppose
that if the frontal sinuses were resonators, the vocal cords would be
strung across them.   It is simply preposterous to suppose that
the frontal sinuses can be resonators to the vocal cords when they
are separated from each other by several inches. The term ' nasal
resonance ' is continually used by a large majority of vocal tutors
because it is found that the phrase begets a good result. The
thoughtful student will realize that ' resonance ' is only intelligible
and reasonable when the frontal and sphenoid sinuses together
with the ethmoid cells are looked upon as the creators of tone,
with the maxillary sinus as resonator. Then we have a compact
machine every detail of which communicates with the nose. Thus

' nasal resonance ' becomes an actual scientific fact, and a matter of definite anatomy, instead of an illogical figure of speech.

The following experiment adds another interesting link in the chain of evidence. In the course of my studies I had a plate made by a dentist which should cover not only the hard and the soft palate of the mouth, but also continue backwards to the naso-pharynx so that the air passing up the windpipe was completely cut off from the nose and the sinuses. The effect upon the tone as I sang was absolutely *nil*. As the air column from the lungs could not reach the sinuses, it was quite clear that they could not be acting as resonators. The volume of tone was unaltered.

At first sight, this experiment seemed also to prove that the vocal cords themselves must be creating the tone. But, on the other hand, there was the fact that people can speak and sing when they have lost the vocal cords, as well as the no less certain fact of their being able to learn to sing on the principles of Sinus Tone Production when the usual methods have absolutely failed.

The position was one of considerable difficulty. The key to the solution of the problem was found in the fact that if, in operations, the vagus nerve be severed high up, the patient invariably loses his voice. We have already seen that this nerve supplies the motive power to all the muscles of the larynx. All that we have to do now is to admit one point, and the mystery is cleared. The solvent—and apparently the only solvent—which can clear the many difficulties with which the subject abounds, and bring into clear harmony the various collected facts, is this, that the nerves themselves are able to set the air in the sinuses vibrating.

Although medical men are usually very unwilling to admit the possibility of this theory, it seems to be the only practical, and, really, the most logical, way out of the apparent maze of contra-dictions with which we appear to be confronted. Indeed, no proof has so far been offered or suggested that can in any way negative the theory.

There can be no question that nerves have important functions in connection with sound vibrations because we depend upon the cochlear division of the eighth or acoustic nerve as the connecting link between that part of the internal ear technically known as the cochlear, and the brain. Without that nerve as a connecting link our brain would be dead to sound ; and we consequently should be utterly deaf.[1]

The nerves are also distinctly affected by sound vibrations, for it has been observed that the reflex movement of the foot, caused by electric stimulus in a chloralized rabbit, is increased when sound is conveyed to the animal's ear.[2]

These facts do not of course *prove* that nerve stimulus can create an air current, the hypothesis is suggested as a possible explanation to those enquirers who have asked, ' What is the initial cause of air movement in the sinuses ? '   Another and more simple explanation is to be found in the reply that the air in our head is under our will control as our hands are, our feet and other parts of our anatomy.

It should be borne in mind that the mere *affirmation* that it is impossible for nerve power to create air currents is no proof of the statement.   In fact the more frequently the nerve theory is put to a practical test by an alert and careful tutor the more obvious does it become that the vocalist has here a possibility of vocal control which heretofore has never been experienced.

It is a fact that ' as men seek, Nature is ever showing them new and unexpected possibilities.'[3]

This matter has fuller consideration in the third volume of this series, namely, *Sinus Tone Production*.

We know that the muscles of our body get their nourishment from the blood, but it is the directing and controlling power of the nerves which enables them to function. We move a book from one place to another. We can only do this through the controlling power which the nerves supply, the origin of control being the grey matter of the brain. This is an accepted procedure recognized by the *cognoscenti*.   What these learned people have not realized is the very simple fact that the air in the cranial sinuses can be brought under the same will control as can our fingers and arms.

The reason is not very clear why from a purely argumentative point of view this new theory should, in the past, have been the subject of so much opposition, for the old and accepted vocal creed, dispassionately considered, is far more difficult of acceptance.

[1] See Appendix J, page 167.
[2] *The Integrative Action of the Nervous System*, by Chas. S. Sherrington, D.Sc., M.D.
[3] *The Gift of Understanding*, essay by Prentice Mulford, Published by Rider & Sons.

It has been believed in the face of manifold contradictions that we are able at will to set our vocal cords at a tension of 1,024 vibrations per second to produce C and 894 vibrations per second to produce A, and so on, without our being in the smallest degree conscious of such proceedings, but a mental shock is produced at the simple proposition that the air in our sinuses is equally under our control as the fingers on our hands.

Who is able to express the limit to which electric agency can be carried ?

Do we not send a message a distance of 4,000 miles without the slightest visible connection with the person who receives it ? What is the thickness of the wall which will prevent an electric message being received on the other side of it, and that, again, without any visible connection being made ? Parenthetically, we may also remark, what student of forty years ago would have believed it possible for a ray of light to pierce completely through wood and iron ? Yet we are now able to make wood as transparent as glass.

Clearly, therefore, for two reasons it would be foolish to say that electrical nervous energy cannot create air vibration. First, because we already have practical experience that such vibrations are possible and under our control ; and second, because we are quite unable to put any limit to the possibilities of electric energy when applied to acoustics.

Moreover, on what ground can we explain the loss of voice which follows the severing of the vagus nerve ? The answer cannot be that it is because the vocal cords have lost their source of energy, for we have already seen that it is possible to speak and sing without this much-discussed part of our anatomy.

There is yet one more and a very interesting reason which upholds the theory of Sinus Tone Production. It is a curious fact, that all the various muscles of the larynx are controlled by the inferior or recurrent laryngeal nerve, excepting one pair, viz., the crico-thyroid, which are supplied by the external branch of the superior laryngeal nerve. Under orthodox theories no explanation can be given why this one set of muscles should have an independent nerve supply. But, if the vocal cords be simply ' breath-governors,' we have a most beautiful and exquisite example of Nature's perfect arrangements for all our wants. We then see that the use of those muscles which are shown in Figure 27 is to control the *amount* of tone, by drawing the cords, either apart from, or towards each other, and so allowing a larger or smaller column of air to pass between them, thus producing either a louder or softer tone.

It is essential that the crico-thyroid muscles should be under separate nerve control, because they will to a large extent control the *pitch* of the tone by directing the column of air from one sinus to another. Hence the crico-thyroid muscles will be able to contract or loosen, and so do their allotted task quite independently of the other muscles.

We can thus—if we have learned the proper control—get any range of *power*, from *pp* to *ff*, by means of the muscles which are supplied by the recurrent laryngeal nerve ; whilst we get our range of pitch very largely through the muscles which are controlled by the external branch of the superior laryngeal nerve. Through this really wonderful arrangement we have the pitch of the note and its volume each under separate nerve control, with a consequent ability to sing every note in the compass of our voice, with every shade of volume.

Although it is not by any means an important point, yet a further link in the chain of evidence is afforded by the fact that very frequently a vibration of the spinal column can be felt when we speak or sing.

Attempts have been made to account for this on the supposition that the air vibrates both above and below the vocal cords, and therefore the spinal column takes its vibrations from the air movement in the lower part of the windpipe. Dr. Aikin says : ' The solid vibrations of the chest, throat, and face are not sources of sound, but are rather the results of strong vibrations of the air column.' Now, we have already shown on page 21 the improbability of the vocal cords creating an air vibration *below* themselves. But the weakness of the suggestion is still further emphasized when we remember that the column of air is enclosed in a narrow tube, the material of which would certainly be a non-conductor of vibrations, as would also the walls of the oesophagus, which intervene between the windpipe and the spine.

Lastly, the air would be travelling in a direction parallel to the spine, and therefore it would have the least possible chance of setting up any vibration there at all.

Now, if we consider the alternative scheme, we know that the vocal cords vibrate when we sing ; we know also that one branch of the spinal accessory nerve arises from the spine, and, through the vagus nerve, is directly connected with the cords themselves. Why, then, should it be thought improbable that these vibrations should be communicated by electrical nerve energy ?

Still keeping a careful watch upon our minds to ensure their freedom from the influence of accepted dogmas, let us see how the matter works out. The food we take sets up a chemical action. Probably no one will be found to deny this proposition.

Speaking at the Royal Artillery Institution, Woolwich, upon ' The Borderland of Chemistry and Electricity,' Mr. William Webster, F.C.S., said : ' This chemical action in the body must produce electricity for it is well known and well proved that chemical action is always co-existent with electrical action.'

Here then, we have electric action set up.

Now, it is universally admitted that the nerves supply power to the muscles. Surely it is reasonable to consider that this electrical action is the self-same power which they supply. We can hardly imagine the nerves supplying power from any other source.

We turn again to Mr. Webster's lecture, and find that he states : ' Light is vibration ; electricity is vibration ; sound is vibration.'

Electricity, then, being vibration, all we have to do is to reduce the power of current which produces bodily movement, and we get air movement, that is, sound, in its place.

How accurately this accords with our knowledge and experience of electric power !

The first submarine cable that was laid between England and America was for a considerable time a failure, because the electricians of that day insisted upon using big induction coils, five feet in length, with currents of very high power. The result was that the high pressure simply made sparks leap through the gutta-percha insulations and so destroy the cable. One of the directors of the cable company was a young man named William Thomson, who had original ideas as to the method that should be used to attain success. He was original enough, and rude enough, to disagree with his co-directors and to tell them that the only possible plan for success was to use a weak current. Sarcastic sneers were the only coin issued as payment for his suggestions. As, however, ' the experts ' continued to fail, and William Thomson—who afterwards became Lord Kelvin—never ceased to proclaim the correctness of his theories, they were eventually tested, and with unqualified success. Thomson *versus* the world of electric experts. Result—victory for Thomson !

How illuminating are these facts in considering the position of speech and song in connection with electrical current !¹ Let the vocalist use too much energy—that is, electric current—and he can ruin both the tone of his voice and the whole of the vocal machinery. On the other hand, reduce the current, and use just enough electric ' vibration ' to communicate a similar vibration to the air which is in the sinuses, and then speech and song of the most beautiful tone are the result.

The theory is completely logical. When more current than it could take was applied to the Atlantic cable, the electricity was bound to find vent somehow, and it did so by bursting through the gutta-percha. When, by our will-power, more electric current is taken up by our nerves than we can use for the purpose of speech or song, that over-supply is bound to find some object on which to fasten, and, of course, the muscles concerned become overtaxed and muscles which, properly, should not be involved at all, are drawn into action, and the whole body, from the hips upwards, becomes more or less a rigid mass.

Here is a lucid and simple explanation of many evils connected with the voice, and it harmonizes with medical experience ; for it has been found in experimenting with frogs, that if the nerve be over-magnetized, it at once becomes rigid.

Two other details, slight perhaps in themselves, yet tending to show a certain similarity in working, may at all events be taken as a ' hint . . . come from Nature.'

(*a*) Helmholtz, in his investigations on the motor nerves of frogs, observed a decided retardation in their conductivity as the effect of cold. It is certainly a matter of common knowledge that a vocalist is unable to do his best if his body be thoroughly cold.

(*b*) Dr. W. Biedermann,² in his book *Electro-Physiology* tells us that ' Sustained pressure and compression of the nerve may seriously injure its conductivity.'

Dealing with vocalism on the lines contained in this chapter, we can easily realize from a medical point of view how essential it is to keep the whole body from head to toe in a complete state of relaxation. Many writers on vocal matters have urged the

¹ See Appendix K, page 169.
² Extraordinary Professor of Physiology in the German University of Prague.

importance of this condition, but here we have a scientific fact, which gives us a clear reason for its observance, namely, that ' sustained pressure injures the conductivity of the nerve.'

Thus we have now a natural law for our guidance instead of merely an *ipse dixit.*

We will now turn to another matter—of deep practical interest. It is a fact that the late Mr. W. Duddell, F.R.S., has shown us not only how we may get musical notes by means of electricity, but on 13th December 1900, at the Institution of Electrical Engineers, he actually played tunes by variations in the power of the electric current. Speaking at the discussion which followed Mr. Duddell's lecture, Professor Ayrton said : ' It was delightful to find a student who so resembled a solid carbon arc that he was ever on the alert to catch at and magnify any hint which may come from Nature or man.'[1]

To the vocalist the above facts are something more than merely a ' hint,' and the ' alert student ' will see in them a definite and concrete proof that electric current can produce musical sounds.

Another ' hint '—and a valuable one, too—comes from Professor Macdonald, who, speaking at Portsmouth in August 1911, said : ' It is still possible that the brain is an instrument, traversed freely as the ear by sound, by an unknown influence which found resonance within it.' This may seem a trifle vague, but it shows that thinking men are getting dissatisfied with the vocal cord theory of tone production, and are beginning to realize how imperfect and illogical are its theories.

A century ago the medical profession had not studied the brain so that definite areas could be considered as responsible for definite work. The brain was as unmapped as the heart of Africa had been a century earlier ; much of the mapping has been proved to be correct, but latterly it has been quite definitely shown that the government of various functions is not as closely confined to special parts as had previously been supposed.

Our specialists tell us that the part of the brain known as Broca's convolution is usually regarded as the speech centre. This detail, however, need not enter into the consideration of the vocal tutor. From the point of view of practical voice control, and bearing in mind the increased brain area which has been attributed of late years to the controlling of specific actions, it will

[1] See Appendix L, page 169.

be helpful to the vocal student to think of the nerve control as coming from the grey matter of the brain at about the skull's centre and from that point to direct the nerve impulses always downwards to points at or between the frontal and sphenoid sinuses, according to the vocal pitch required.

A ship having been built on certain theories is only *known* to be sound in all its parts after its test at the trial trip. So, this vocal system has been built up upon certain theories. Up to the present (January 1938) the practical results have not only proved the theories to be correct, but have by a long way exceeded even the most sanguine expectations.

We have, however, not yet completed our theories. In the address given by Sir William Crookes, F.R.S., V.P.C.S., as President of the British Association for the Advancement of Science, in 1898, the following statements occur : ' It is supposed by some physiologists that the essential cells of nerves do not actually touch, but are separated by a narrow gap which widens in sleep, while it narrows almost to extinction during the mental activity. This condition is singularly like that of a Branly or Lodge coherer.'

Two more details and our electric theories are finished.

First, the bone which forms the upper part of the frontal sinus has many lines or ridges upon it. So far as we know there is no text-book of anatomy which gives any name to, or reason for, these ridges. It is not, therefore, unreasonable to suggest that their office might be to collect the electric vibrations in a way similar to that of an aerial in wireless telegraphy.

Second, the two nerves, the vagus and the spinal accessory, travel together in the same sheath at their entrance to the brain. As there are not any other nerves which travel in this way, we must certainly conclude that Nature has some useful purpose to serve in thus placing them together. Is it not possible that by their juxtaposition they may perhaps act in a manner somewhat similar to the wires of an electric light ? The results of certain experiments add a degree of probability to this suggestion. The experiments in question go to show that in sleep the nerve fibres separate, but in consciousness they meet again. That is to say, in activity the nerve fibres are in touch with each other, but in unconsciousness they are separated. So, in a similar manner, it would appear that the vagus nerve and the spinal accessory meet in phonation, but are apart in silence.

Now let us piece and fit together the various facts and ideas contained in this chapter, and see how wonderfully the idea of electric power in vocalization harmonizes with our present knowledge of the subject in the realms of physics.

We have the mixing of various chemicals in the body, taken in the shape of food. These chemical mixtures produce a power which we may call electric, for it is admitted that there is a strong analogy between nervous action and electricity. This particular power is taken up by the nerves and supplied to the muscles to produce bodily movement.

The same power, in a weakened form, produces air movement, that is ' voice.' It is only an ' extremely feeble electric stimulus ' that will produce the required results in the coherers designed for wireless telegraphy by Sir Oliver Lodge and other scientists. A strong current is fatal ; so is it in speech.

Thus, the work of the voice trainer centres around the fact that an ' extremely feeble electric stimulus ' applied through the brain and the nerves to the air in the sinuses creates good tone. Put this statement by the side of Professor Macdonald's ' hint ' on page 109, and it will be seen that the two have much in common.

The whole message of this book is to show that it is impossible for soft material (which will of course include brain as well as vocal cords) to produce tone. Hence the brain cannot be ' an instrument traversed freely as the ear by sound ' ; but it is possible[1] that nerve contact taking place in the brain, the nervous power is there created which produces the air movement in the sinuses which we denominate vocal tone. It assuredly has been proved up to the very hilt, that simple directions for the guidance of the student can be formulated on these lines,·which give a complete and eminently satisfactory control of the voice, the mind guiding it with unerring precision.

To explain in a book to the reader exactly *how* this is accomplished would be impossible. The lesson can be given only in person. The mere possession of Dent's *First Steps in French* would never teach the owner to speak the French language. The sounds formed by the student must be heard and corrected by a competent tutor.

Under such trustworthy guidance, singing becomes a matter of accurate management, and with persistent repetition the accurate

[1] The author, and many others with him, believe it is certain.

management becomes a well established habit. The charm and simplicity of the work form a tremendous contrast to the accepted theories which include ' mixed ' voice, ' chest ' voice, ' middle ' voice, ' head ' voice, ' chink of the glottis,' ' shock of the glottis,' and many other terms equally vague and confusing !

No wonder that people are beginning to realize, although many will not own it, that our text-books contradict each other, that our theories are illogical, and that the practical results which are produced are very frequently far from being satisfactory.

The Right Hon. W. E. Gladstone, in writing a survey of the half-century which closed in 1887, said : ' All science seems to be reconsidering its position. The conclusions which satisfied our fathers and our younger selves are sternly questioned.'

Think what magnificent results have been obtained by those who have ' sternly questioned ' the facts of science as then understood !

Consider the saving of human life effected by wireless telegraphy and by the Röntgen rays. Calculate, if possible, the accumulated hours, amounting to years upon years, spent by the chemist in the laboratory, with the result that we now know that our food supply will always be abundant, and so will the sources of energy.

If such were our object, we could write many chapters upon such thoughts and accomplishments.

Our present object, however, is an earnest plea for a reconsideration of the position of vocalization and speech, not because of any pecuniary advantage which might accrue to the author of this work by the acceptance of its theories, but because experience has proved that it will add another item to the advantage of the human race both from a positive and also from a negative point of view, inasmuch as an acceptance of its doctrines will not only provide beauty of voice, but also prevent a loss of voice with all its attendant miseries.

It must be admitted that one other point is in the mind of the author, and that a patriotic one. He knows, and is fully assured, that the vocal cords do not themselves produce tone. This he is convinced is *the truth*, and truth cannot die.

But we also know that Professor D. E. Hughes, the famous London man of science, was the first inventor of a coherer, but when he brought his wonderful invention to the notice of our Royal Society, the scientific committee, led by Sir George Stokes and Professor Huxley, so discouraged him in his marvellous experiments that he let the whole matter drop. Years afterwards, Professor Righi designed another apparatus, and so the ground lost in England in 1879 was afterwards regained—abroad ! Is this to be the fate of my studies and experiments ? Probably not, if the practical value of the work is realized, and also how infinitely more wonderful the voice is when considered from this new standpoint.

We have the air obeying acoustic laws, the nerves obeying electric laws, and our osseous anatomy conforming to musical laws.

According to vocal cord theories, it is difficult, if not impossible, to find any known law which is kept. How true and beautiful are the words of Sir William Crookes : '. . . Steadily, unflinchingly, we strive to pierce the inmost heart of Nature, . . . Veil after veil we have lifted, and her face grows more beautiful, august and wonderful with every barrier that is withdrawn.'

The voice as a wind instrument is infinitely more wonderful than as a vocal cord instrument. It has been well said that ' science never destroys wonder but only shifts it higher and deeper.'[1] This has been verified in an extraordinary manner in the gradual but increasing growth of the art of Sinus Tone Production since it was first launched upon the musical and scientific world in 1909. Since then height upon height has been realized and one is reminded of Emerson's beautiful picture of a little child looking upwards through the maple branches.

> Over his head were the maple buds,
> And over the tree was the moon ;
> And over the moon were the starry studs
> That drop from the angels' shoon.

---

[1] *Introduction to Science*, by the late Sir J. A. Thomson.

I

CHAPTER VI

VENTRICULAR BANDS

Truth is always present; it only needs to lift the iron lids of
the mind's eye to read its oracles.—EMERSON.

THIS chapter, as also Chapter V, deals with points chiefly
theoretical, and therefore may be passed over by those who prefer
to deal only with the practical side of the question. From that
point of view, all has been said that is necessary for the happy and
easy production of good vocal tone; but in order that all the
irregular straws of our irregular art may be placed in systematic
and orderly regularity, we will now consider the functions and the
possibilities of that vexatious and illusive part of our anatomy
known as the false vocal cords, or ventricular bands.

Many and ingenious have been the theories advanced as to the
utilitarian position they occupy in the economy of Nature's plans,
but in the opinion of the present writer the authors have all fallen
short of success, because they have each endeavoured to form and
even twist Nature's facts into such shapes as will harmonize with
and support their own particular ideas instead of first getting at
the root of the difficulty, and then, with careful thought, grafting
all other work upon it.

This course frequently means disappointment after disappointment, as the writer knows to his cost, for difficulties and unexpected
issues arise with which the mind of the searcher had not reckoned,
and these may possibly appear to wreck the whole of his previous
work. In such a case, the only plan of action is to endeavour to
discover the flaw in the logic which has upset the equilibrium of
the scheme, and then to start work again. Many years of patient
thought and earnest care have usually thus to be spent by the
searcher for *truth*, in the endeavour to piece together the different
facts of his subject, so as eventually to form a sound and reliable
whole.

It has been well said that 'science, so long as it is true to itself
must ignore and despise no order of facts. Its object is truth, of
which all facts are part. . . . If there is apparent contradiction,

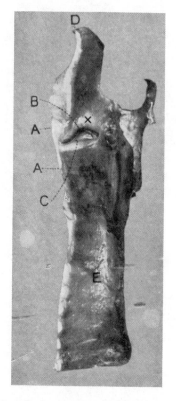

FIGURE 28. WINDPIPE WITH THE TRUE AND FALSE VOCAL
CORDS

it must be faced, with the full assurance that it is only apparent, and that truth lies in the explanation, whatever it be.'

Two cases of ingenious argument, but with a serious flaw in each, have already been quoted.[1] It would be well here to mention another. A very prominent writer and teacher is now referred to, who insisted that the use of the false vocal cords was to assist the work of the true cords (situated just below them) by creating a *backward* air current, and thus counteracting to some extent the upward breath pressure upon them from below. In order that the argument may be completely understood, let the reader refer to Figure 28.

The breath coming up the windpipe from the lungs, meets with its first obstruction at the vocal cords. But a second resistance (so this particular author states) is met at the false vocal cords just above, so that a current of air is sent back again towards the true cords. Such a theory may be clever and ingenious, but it completely breaks down in practice, because the false cords never approximate in phonation as the true cords do, and therefore it is a physical impossibility for them either to control or offer any material resistance to the air which has already passed its first obstruction.

The true key to the situation is to be found in the *arched* shape of the false cords, a fact which the author just quoted altogether ignores, whilst other points are much exaggerated. It is hoped that by reference to the accompanying photograph a true and correct impression of the anatomy of the larynx and the region surrounding it may be conveyed to the reader's mind. The picture shows the right half of the windpipe and vocal cords. *A A* is the thyroid cartilage, which, with its corresponding half, forms the angle known as Adam's apple. *B* is the false vocal cord, or ventricular band, also known as the superior thyro-arytenoid ligament. *C* is the true vocal cord, fixed at one end to the thyroid cartilage. *D* is the epiglottis. In the act of swallowing this falls backwards— that is, towards the right in the picture—so preserving to the windpipe a freedom from foreign substances. *E* is the windpipe.

Behind the false cords a small passage known as the sacculus laryngis, or laryngeal pouch,[2] goes upward, forming a kind of closed chimney. Now, the consideration of these details, and the

[1] See pages 42 and 69.
[2] Also termed the appendix ventriculi laryngis.

endeavour to ascertain their possible meaning, has doubtless been the cause of much searching and anxious thought to many minds ; but no real success has been attained. In Morris's *Treatise on Anatomy* it is stated : ' In man the function of the laryngeal pouches, besides that of pouring out the secretion of the glands located within their walls, is not known.' This lack of knowledge is probably due to the fact that the searchers have tried to solve the enigma by making an imaginary connection between the true cords and the false cords above them. It is by no means certain that any such connection exists. In the first edition of this work, a suggestion was made as follows as to the probable use of the false cords, and there does not appear to be any necessity to withdraw it. The interior arch, or we might call it the closed top of the chimney, will in its natural state of necessity be self-supporting, and also carry the weight which is directly above it. Now, under certain conditions one is able to let the muscles of the arch cease from activity.[1] That is, we can allow them to be in a loose, flaccid condition, when the weight of the structure falls from the point X, that is *about* where the top of the closed chimney would be (the position varies a great deal in different people), to the point indicated at the lowest end of the dotted B line, *i.e.*, upon the centre of the arch, or, in other words, upon the centre of the false vocal cords, and this weight is bound to travel to the extremity of the arch at either end.

What now, is the practical result of all this ? It will be seen as follows. In rapid vocal passages the interior arch of the sacculus laryngis indicated at X and the arch of the false cords shown at the lower end of the line at B (with the corresponding arches on the left side of the windpipe) support all weight above them, leaving the whole length of the vocal cords the utmost freedom of movement, but when the cords require to be held for the time being in one position, as they do when one steady note is sung, then, the vocal cords being placed so as to allow the requisite amount of air for tone production to pass between them, the arch shown at X at once automatically ceases from activity, when weight falls upon the centre of the false vocal cord arch, and thence to its extreme points, where the pressure—small though it would

---

[1] In a somewhat similar way the pianist is—or should be—able to allow the muscles of the arm either to support the arm weight, or to cease from supporting it, as occasion may require.

be—would keep the vocal cord extremities in position with perfect ease whilst their middle parts would remain absolutely elastic, and thus allow the air column to pass smoothly between them. Thus, instead of having any strain upon the delicate elastic muscles which guide and control the cords, they are simply held in position, for the production of the before-mentioned long note, by mere weight from above, thus relieving the muscles of undue tension. A simile—although an imperfect one—may be found in the action of a tennis racquet press. The screws of the press answer for the weight above, and by their use strain is taken off the racquet, and it is kept in position and good order.

The whole of this *arch* theory seems to the writer an exquisite matter of beautiful balance ; and while it is in complete accord with the theory of ' downward thought ' (see page 37), yet it in no way militates against the school of ' equipoise,' or equal balance of all parts. Thus the idea seems to coincide with the arrangements with which Nature has provided us, and it does not raise any question as to physical possibilities. The laws of construction as laid out in mechanics are also in harmony with the scheme, while it also agrees *practically* with the pet theories of more than one popular voice trainer. It would be difficult, and perhaps impossible, quite definitely to prove that these ideas are correct, but they certainly work well in practice.

Since writing the above, another and more obvious use can be placed to the credit of this anatomical puzzle, which bears the impress of truth from the standpoint of physics, anatomy, and practice. Let us take the practical side first.

If a person has to lift or push a heavy weight, the first movement is invariably to take a big breath, and then to imprison the air, so that it does not escape until the weight has been released from the body. Such a course of action is practically automatic and unconscious with all men when special physical exertion is required. What are the anatomical facts which correspond with and make possible these actions ? The ribs rise, the big breath fills the lungs, the chest cavity becomes packed with air. The laryngeal pouches then become inflated with the pneumatic pressure, and by reference to Figure 29 it will be readily seen that the greater the upward pressure, the tighter are the interior walls of the pouches pressed to each other, so that the outward passage of the air is firmly blocked, and the secretions from the glands would help to make the passage completely air-tight. In a word, the air passage would be sealed. With such an upward tension it is, from a mechanical point of view, absolutely essential to have a fixed and firm basis at the opposite end of the air column. This is exactly what Nature has given us, and that in a very wonderful manner. In easy and ordinary breathing the lungs are quite free at their base, but in forced breathing they touch and rest upon the diaphragm, which is attached to the spine. Thus, one extremity of the strain is taken by the laryngeal pouches and the other end by the spine; but inasmuch as fluids press equally in all directions, it follows that the pressure is also spread over the whole of the chest walls.

When a football is kicked the strain is not taken entirely where the foot makes the point of impact with the ball, but is distributed over its whole surface. Now let us turn to Figure 28, and see how beautifully the false cords and the pouches are formed for their purpose. The false cords make a firm and strong edge at the entrance of the pouch (that is to say, at the lower and free end of the chimney indicated by the lower end of the line B), so that the inner and outer walls shall not be able to touch each other, and the air will therefore have quite an easy access to the pouch. Without the slight ridge which the false cords create, the membrane which forms the inner wall of the pouch would have been liable to adhere to the membrane forming the outer wall, and so the entrance would have been either partially or entirely blocked, and the whole mechanism rendered inoperative.

An air-tight passage is thus secured by means of the false cords, and the requisite pressure made available, for the purposes of vomiting and defaecation.

In the latter action, the closing and the pressure at the throat is easily noticed when any extra or special pressure is used. Moreover, a comparison of the structure of the true cords with the false, and their respective surroundings, is a matter of no small interest. The true cords are composed of yellow elastic tissue, and are capable of very quick, ready and varied movement, but with a mechanism that would be obviously incapable of bearing the slightest strain. The false cords are considerably less elastic, and certain white *fibrous* tissue and its fibres extend upwards from the cords into the walls of the pouch, or chimney, thus

giving a considerable amount of additional strength to that part
which would specially need it.

Figure 29 shows the difference in the pouch under normal
conditions and when in a state of air pressure. The left-hand side
shows the chimney in a state of relaxation, and on the right we
see its elongated position under air pressure. It is evident that

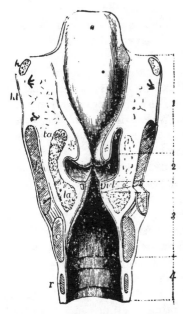

FIGURE 29. SECTION OF LARYNX

On the left is the laryngeal pouch in a state of rest ; and on the right the
pouch under air pressure (S, S¹). When pressure is used both sides
become elongated, as shown on the right-hand side of the picture.[1]

this lengthening of the chimney gives a larger surface wherewith
to effect a complete closing of the air passage just above the true
vocal cords, and we need only release the activity of the walls
which form the chimney, and the whole passage at once becomes
free again.

Surely the person must be blind indeed who fails to see here
the exquisite balance and perfect arrangements of Nature for our

[1] Taken from *Quain's Anatomy*, Vol. II, Part 2, and reproduced
by kind permission of Longmans, Green & Co.

well-being. ' It is order, sequence and interchange of application which is mighty in Nature,' wrote Francis Bacon, and that truth is made very evident in considering the details just set forth.

In *Quain's Anatomy* (Vol. II, Part 2) the following passage occurs :—' Wylie showed (*Edinburgh Mediccl Journal*, 1866) that when the plicae ventriculares ' (*i.e.*, false vocal cords) ' are simply approximated, and air is injected into the larynx from below, they prevent the exit of the air, and he held that the closure of the glottis in defaecation and vomiting is mainly effected by their apposition. His experiments have been confirmed by Brunton and Cash.'

A passing statement such as this does but little justice to the wonderful beauty and fitness of this tiny portion of our breathing apparatus. One can also see by the wording of the statement that the experimenter (Wylie) did not appreciate the full importance of his deduction in the matter, for, as we have just seen, the closure of the glottis in defaecation is not ' mainly' but *entirely* effected by their apposition, and that because the true vocal cords are utterly unsuitable for any such work.

We have yet one more point of view to discuss, namely, the physical side. Why should we always take a big breath before making a physical exertion ? The question may possibly be capable of several answers ; but one reply is, that by so doing we get additional power from the compressed air within us.

The breath is always taken when our position is erect, because in this position we can inhale the largest possible amount of air. We then assume a bending attitude, and in so doing can get an air compression which naturally tends to straighten our body again, and when this is accomplished we have lifted or moved the weight, and we have gained our end.

CHAPTER VII

INHALATION AND ENUNCIATION

Men are apt to prefer a prosperous error to an
inflicted truth.—JEREMY TAYLOR.

THE NECESSITIES of this chapter are but small. A large majority
of singing masters and books on singing regard the term *breathing*
as applying to inhalation only, whereas it must be perfectly
obvious to anyone who considers the matter, that breathing
consists firstly of taking in a breath, and secondly of letting it out.
Now, although it is contrary to the usually accepted ideas on the
matter, the former is comparatively speaking of but little importance, the whole art and science of singing rests upon the latter,
i.e., exhalation. The designer of a locomotive would probably not
give a vast deal of thought to the building and shape of the water
tank, or the method in which it should be filled. His skill and art
consist in arranging how the water (in the form of steam) should
leave the engine, and its action in so doing. I am, of course, quite
aware that there is a huge difference between the human form
and a locomotive, but many valuable lessons may be learnt from
things which in themselves are dissimilar, *e.g.*, the keyhole of a
door and the art of singing. So we may use the locomotive as a
kind of picture to show us that infinitely more skill and attention
are required for letting breath out than for taking it in. Chapters
II and III have been devoted to the former. Chapter VII will
give a little advice on the latter subject.

In the opinion of some masters, it is a matter of no importance
how the breath is taken in or by what method we fill our lungs.
As, however, there *should* be method in everything even to the
smallest details of life, we will proceed to examine those plans
which exist in relation to the matter.

So far as I am aware, there are only three different systems of
inhalation. The first is known as the clavicular. This consists in
raising the clavicles, *i.e.*, the collar bones and the shoulder blades
as breath is taken in. This system is fortunately, very little
taught, for it is very ugly, and I have never been able to find any
advantage from such an action in breathing. The plan which is

largely followed is the abdominal system, that is, breathing as low as possible, the reason given being that the lungs are broader at their base than they are at the top.

That fact is undoubtedly true, but the lungs can be better filled both at the base and on the top, on another principle, known as the lateral-costal, and students would do well to work on these lines.

To put the matter tersely, though I hope clearly, the lungs are known to be enclosed within the ribs ; that is to say, the ribs form a kind of outer guard to the lungs. Now when the abdominal muscles are drawn inwards as a breath is taken, the ribs at once rise, leaving the lungs free to expand to their utmost. This, in the author's opinion, is undoubtedly the best system of inhalation. Those who wish to go further into small details of the subject should get Dr. Hulbert's book on *Breathing* (Novello & Co.), where the matter is dealt with at some length, and some thirty-seven exercises on breathing, or, rather, on inhalation, are given. Personally, I always find that two or three exercises at the outside are all that are required and answer every purpose. Moreover, a pupil will practise two or three exercises, perhaps, but if one asks for thirty-seven to be practised, it sounds a decidedly big request.

An exercise which pupils have found very useful, is taken as follows : Let the student stand in an easy, erect position, with the hands flat down by the sides, the tips of the middle fingers coming almost to the sides of the knee. Get the lungs fairly empty, then begin the exercise by taking a slow breath through the nostrils, gradually extending the arms from position *A* to position *B*, in which the palm of the hand is towards the floor.

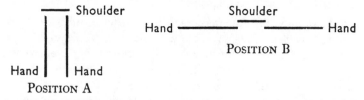

By the time that the hands are on a level with the shoulder the lungs should be full. Having arrived at this position, suddenly expel the breath as quickly and as fully as possible out of the nose and mouth, at the same time turning the palms of the hands upward towards the ceiling. The lungs having been emptied, the second inhalation is taken very slowly through the nostrils only, the hands at the same time being gradually raised until the fingers can meet above the head in position indicated by *C*, by which time the lungs should be full. Do not on any account make even

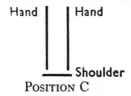

POSITION C

the smallest pause in this position, but at *once* slowly return to position *B*, exhaling at the same time. By the time that the hands are on a level with the shoulder (the palms being upwards), the lungs should be empty. Then reverse the position of the hands and slowly inhale through the nostrils, keeping the arms extended as at *B*, with the palms of the hands towards the floor. When the lungs are full, let the hands slowly descend, keeping the arms fully stretched, and exhale slowly through mouth and nose until the original position is reached, when the lungs should be *well* emptied so that it is necessary to take a big breath as a relief.

The last part is the most important, as the weight of the extended arms and hands in descending should help to empty the lungs, as completely as possible. The second part of the exercise, in which the hands and arms are extended above the head, should not be taken by anyone who has a weak heart. For such a person the first and last movements will suffice. But a small amount of time need be devoted to these exercises. The complete exercise should be performed very slowly indeed, about three or four times the first thing in the morning and the last thing at night. This will take less than ten minutes out of the day, but if performed with regularity, a considerable benefit will accrue, both as regards the length of time and ease with which the outgoing breath can be controlled, and also with respect to general health.

The student will find also that there will be less difficulty in taking a long breath quickly. To be able to do this is frequently a very important matter in singing. It is, perhaps, almost unnecessary to remark that one's ordinary inhalations should be carried on through the nostrils only. As a matter of general health, this is important, so that the air may be purified and

warmed by passing through the nostrils before entering the windpipe and lungs.

The question has been asked by students : ' Should the lungs
be expanded by a lateral and downward motion, or should they
be allowed to expand also towards the front and back and upwards ? ' The correct answer to this question is : ' Let them
expand *naturally* in every direction, in just the same way as when
a sponge is put into water it swells on every side.' It should be
borne in mind that the five lobes of our lungs in their natural
condition are already filled with air. The extra amount that is
really required for singing purposes is very small ; in fact, a
much smaller amount than is usually considered necessary ; and
especially is this the case in the early stages of a pupil's career.
The method of taking the additional supply should be by gently
lifting the ribs away from the lungs by a slight drawing in of the
abdominal muscles. The weight of the ribs is lifted, and the lungs
expand as the air flows in.

Although it is a matter of common knowledge, there can be
no harm in remarking upon the importance of quiet breathing.
Heavy and laboured breathing is always an abomination, without
the smallest possible advantage of any kind. The Latin proverb,
ars est celare artem (the art is to hide art), holds true with respect
to singing as much as, and perhaps more than, in any other
department of skill.

Many will, doubtless, disagree with the theories for voice-
production which this work sets forth, but a well-known writer
says : ' In the battle of science it has always been one against a
multitude, and is even so in our own day.' There will, however,
be no dissentient to the remark that it is one of the sweetest and
happiest experiences possible, to listen to a song—be it ever so
simple—delivered with good tone, good enunciation, with absolute
ease and grace, and sung from the heart. This is a truism which
no one will combat.

Those who take the trouble to work on the lines enunciated
in this book, and these lines distinctly spell hard work, will find
that eventually singing with grace and ease, from the heart, is
comparatively easy, because *all* physical work has been eliminated.
Such a statement may appear untrue and even impossible, judging
by even our very best artists. In support, therefore, of my assertion, let me take what is exactly a parallel case, viz., the act of

pianoforte playing. I will again quote Mr. Tobias Matthay—he says :

The supposition that tone production at the pianoforte should be attained by any real unmitigated hitting or striking at the keys is a fallacy that has probably arisen, like so many other indefensible dogmas relating to pianoforte technique, owing to the initial mistake—that of studying the *visible* effects—of the limb movements, etc., that accompany correct production—instead of studying the laws involved in the use of the pianoforte key itself and the muscular condition of the implicated limbs.

This is exactly analogous to what has taken and is taking place with respect to singing. The student goes to a concert and hears one of our best singers. Apparently, a big breath is taken before attempting a top note, and this note, when reached, is accompanied by a certain dramatic movement which is mistaken for an exertion, but is really not one at all. The tyro gets a copy of the same music and endeavours at home to sing it in the same way. The biggest possible breath is taken when approaching the high note, and then when the tremendous moment arrives every muscle that can possibly be brought to bear is used and strained to the utmost, in the terrific and, it must be owned, courageous attempt to get that note by hook or by crook. Poor thing, poor thing ! If only you would ' study the laws involved in the use of the ' voice, how differently would you act ! The artist whom you so admired at the concert certainly took a big breath, but that breath was not brought into action all at once. It was the tiniest possible stream of air that was being used, but the note being a high one, the movement of the air column was exceedingly rapid, hence the necessity for a long breath to complete the phrase, and what you mistook for a physical exertion was simply a dramatic movement which quite correctly accompanied a dramatic ending to the song.

Of course, it goes without saying that the laws involved in the use of the voice are numerous, and the ways in which vocalists may go wrong are simply legion. For those who are trying to help themselves by means of this book, the following simple and practical summary of certain acoustic laws may be useful.

In passing from low notes to high notes, there are three important factors for the student to bear in mind, viz. :

1. The position
2. The shape } of the breath.
3. The pressure

The position for the breath movement should be more forward.

The shape of the breath should be smaller.[1]

The pressure of the breath should be less.

Here, again, we have another threefold cord, and careful attention to it will carry the student a very considerable distance along the line of progress towards his desired goal.

In the *Daily Chronicle* for Wednesday 20th October 1909 appeared a review of a book by Agnes Murphy, entitled *A Sweet Singer*. This is a biography of Madame Melba. The reviewer—George Sampson—expresses himself in the following original manner. He says :

Her voice has mechanical perfection, and mechanical perfection is a very great deal, for it is always reliable. I could hardly trust any man as implicitly as I trust the Goertz lens on my camera, and yet just as the human eye is all that a lens is, and something much more, so Melba's voice has that comforting, reliable perfection of mechanism with the something much more that human intelligence and feeling can add to it.

Now it is remarkable how the phrase ' comforting, reliable perfection of mechanism ' is applicable to the work which this volume describes. When a piece of machinery is out of order, an engineer would be called in to find out where the fault lies. Having examined it, he would probably loosen one screw, or tighten another, would lengthen one arm or shorten another, and having absolutely adjusted every part, the machine would once again be capable of smoothly doing its work. So should it be with the vocalist. A singer comes to a master for help, and on the lines laid down here, the practised ear can detect the precise cause of each separate fault, and the master's knowledge and experience as a teacher will enable him to give such directions to his pupil as will clear away every difficulty.

The idea of reliable mechanism is also useful, because we know that the same machine under the same conditions will always produce the same result.

It is not sufficient that the would-be vocalist shall learn to produce flawless tone—it is the teacher's duty to acquaint him with the exact steps and process necessary for its production. It is not enough to sing well, one should also know *how* one does it. When this has been accomplished, the vocalist is the happy possessor of a ' reliable mechanism ' of which he is the complete master.

Francis Bacon, Lord Verulam, at the beginning of the seventeenth

[1] See manometric flames, page 30.

century wrote : ' The true kind of experience is not the mere groping of a man in the dark, who feels at random to find his way, instead of waiting for the dawn or striking a light, . . . it begins with an ordered—not chaotic—arrangement of facts, deduces axioms from them, and from the axioms again designs new experiments.' This is exactly where the strength of Sinus Tone Production lies. The plans we have been unfolding are capable of dethroning the goddess of Empiricism, who has only too long held sway over our noble art, and in her place shall be set up a government, guided and controlled by science and skill, which shall give the earnest student the certainty that he may grow into the beautiful maturity of the polished and finished artist.

There is nothing new to say with respect to enunciation in singing, but as it is hoped that this book may be used by beginners, as well as by the advanced vocalist, it will be well to make it fairly complete, although in doing so, this part of the ground has already been well trodden by others who are thoroughly com petent to speak upon the subject.

There are two important rules to bear in mind with respect to consonants. In words that begin with a consonant, it will frequently be found of great help to treat the first consonant very lightly, and to get as quickly as possible on to the vowel sound. If the consonant be emphasized, the doing so frequently throws back the vowel sound, whereas, of course, it should come as far forward as possible.

When two of the same consonants come together one is often made to do double duty, e.g., ' Love was not felt till noble heart beat high.' Unless great care is exercised, the fourth and fifth words will run into one—*feltill*. In order to avoid this, the tongue must drop from the roof of the mouth when it forms the first *t before* it begins the word ' till.' Similar carelessness is often experienced in joining a final consonant on to the vowel sound of the next word ; thus—' and eyes of blue ' becomes ' ari deyes of blue,' which is a very different matter. Watch closely that the vowel *e* is not drawn into the sound *i*, for instance, is frequently sung In order to avoid the two vowel sounds, the mouth must be kept in exactly the same position for the second note as for the first. It will be noticed that *Li eght* is produced by a gradual closing of the mouth, which, of course, is wrong. There are, too, many words which require more careful treatment in singing than is frequently bestowed upon them in speech. Be careful that the last syllable of *roses* is *es*, not *is*. Be careful that the last syllable of *righteous* is *teous* not *chus*. Be careful that the last syllable of *shepherd* is *herd* not *erd*. Be careful that the last sound of *and* is *d*, not *n*. Be sure that all words which end with a consonant have the final sound clearly articulated.

Whilst dealing with this part of our subject, a further point of interest and also of usefulness should have consideration, that is, the analysis of speech.

Two and often three factors are employed in the production of speech, viz., (*a*) the pitch of the sound, that is, the vibrating element itself ; (*b*) the vowel-tone ; with frequently the addition of (*c*) consonant-sound. Each of these divisions has its own particular machinery for production, and therefore, demands distinct and separate attention from both student and master.

As we have already seen the air movement in the sinuses creates tone. Here, then, we get pitch.

The vowel sounds depend simply upon the shape of the mouth.

Ah is formed by dropping the jaw and allowing the tongue to lie flat and loosely in the mouth.

Then, by drawing the lips together and pushing them slightly forward, we get *oo*, as in ' food.'

O comes by slightly opening the lips while they are in the same forward position.

Again, starting with *ah* as our ground-work, if we widen the tongue, the *ah* changes to *eh*, as in ' pet,' and a still further widening produces *ee*, as in ' feet.'

This, of course, does not, by a very long way, cover the whole possibilities of vowel sounds, but it is sufficient to show that they are made by simply altering the shape of the mouth cavity, and, therefore, the compass of the voice which is possible for *ah* should be, and would be, possible for other vocal sounds, providing no muscular contraction interferes with the free passage of the air through the sinuses. Let a pupil fully realize this, and many difficulties will disappear.

The letter *h* before a vowel requires at times very careful treatment, and for this very interesting reason : An aspirate is formed by allowing the breath to escape out of the mouth. One cannot sing on an aspirate ; vocalization can only be obtained on the

vowel which follows it. Take for example the word he. The
musical sound only can commence when we reach *e*. In the word
who, real tone is only made on *oo*, not on *wh*. An aspirate then
tends to misdirect the breath for singing, because the air in the
sinuses is not set into movement. Frequently, therefore, it will
be found very helpful to minimize the force and character of the
h sound, so far as may be done without damage to our language,
in order to keep the breath moving in the higher cavities.

Consonants are formed by either a partial or complete blocking
of the air column at the lips or by the tongue and the posterior
part of the nose.

F is formed by placing the lower lip against the upper teeth,
and so breaking up the air column.

S is made by placing the tongue against the roof of the mouth,
and so *partially* closing the breath passage.

When the passage is completely blocked in the mouth and at
the nose, then we get *t* upon the release of the air.

A similar movement produces *d*.

N is made by the same position as regards the mouth, but with
an open passage at the nose.

M also requires a free nasal passage, but with the lips quite
closed.

B has the same lip position as *m*, but the nasal passage must be
closed, and the *b* is formed when the lips separate.

It is hardly necessary to go through all the consonant sounds
in this manner; enough has been said to show the threefold
nature of speech.

When we come to a song, there are two additional points to
consider, namely, time and melody. A difficult musical passage
may frequently be dealt with successfully by taking each factor
entirely by itself, and afterwards uniting them one by one until
the whole is complete.

When this has been done, the artistic side of the poem which
is being studied should claim attention.

A few words with respect to the amount of time devoted to
practising may not be amiss. The best time, if it can be managed,
is about twenty or thirty minutes before a meal. A robust voice
may practise for one and a half hours every day, the time being
divided into four or more equal sections. A weaker voice should
be satisfied with one hour divided into three equal parts, of which

K

not less than forty-five minutes should be devoted to technical exercises (not vocalizes).

Whilst fully recognizing the fact that voices cannot be fully developed either by post or by book, yet it is sincerely hoped that the ideas set forth in this volume will be found of considerable value to vocalists and also to those who train them.

As a matter of fact, the first edition of this book proved that these hopes were well founded, for the most sanguine expectations of the writer were surpassed.

The author is aware that the acceptance of the theories will mean a very considerable revision of medical works, and also of medical practice, with respect to the voice, but it will surely be admitted that finality has not yet been reached in medical any more than in botanical or any other branch of science. All he asks is that the matter shall be approached with an open mind, that the possibility of the statements shall have fair consideration, and that the whole system be treated on its merits. That it possesses the merits claimed for it can easily be proved (see pages 15 and 82).[1] Whether they will be generally acknowledged, time alone will show.

I once had a very excellent piece of advice given to me by a friend[2] (I use the term ' friend ' in its highest and best sense), which, although it may seem simple and obvious enough, yet has in a variety of ways proved of very great value. It was : ' Never take a thing for granted.' I would ask my readers to treat the contents of this book in the same spirit. Let each one make a personal test of the statements made ; do not be satisfied merely to accept the opinions of other people, unless you are quite incompetent to form your own. Let the opinions of other people have due consideration, but do not let that suffice, for by so doing you take for granted that individual attention to the question is not required. Had Dr. (afterwards Sir James) Simpson so acted, the benefits of chloroform in surgery might never have been known. Had Sir Charles Parsons so acted, the turbine engine might never have ploughed the Atlantic. Shall I be accused of egotism if I add—had I so acted, I should have been content to work on the same lines as my predecessors, thus the knowledge

[1] Considerable further testimony is given in the Second Volume of this series. *Light on the Voice Beautiful* (6/-).

[2] The late Rev. W. Dodge, B.A., 25 years Vicar of St. Stephen's Church, Southwark.

and the possibilities of head or Sinus Tone Production would at all events have been delayed.

That the possibilities are great is at present known to but comparatively few, but I live in the hope that before many years have passed the throat and vocal cords as sound producers will be cleared out ' bag and baggage,' to use Mr. Gladstone's well-known formula, from all voice training, because it will be realized that they are as feeble a means for producing sound as implements of the Stone Age would now be considered feeble for producing power and that throughout the world everyone with power of speech and vocalization will be making use of and acknowledging the benefits of head or Sinus Tone Production.

In a letter addressed to John Daniel Horst,[1] written from London in February 1654/5, Dr. William Harvey said : ' Nor do I doubt but that many things still lie hidden in Democritus's well that are destined to be drawn up into the light by the indefatigable diligence of coming ages.' I trust that posterity, and perhaps even my own generation, will eventually admit that I have drawn up one truth from that well ' by indefatigable diligence.' ' With what labour do we attain to the hidden things of truth,' writes the same surgeon in another letter ; but it is probably only those who have themselves spent years in the endeavour to unravel a complicated idea who can quite realize what concentration and energy are necessary to accomplish successfully the self-imposed task.

---

[1] Principal Physician at the Court of Hesse-Darmstadt.

CHAPTER VIII
THE ARTIST

To keep in sight Perfection, and adore
The vision, is the artist's best delight.—SIR WILLIAM WATSON.

HEINRICH HEINE was one day walking with a friend in the city of Amiens. Whilst admiring the beauty and magnificence of the cathedral, he said to his companion, ' This building was not created by opinion, it was built through conviction.'

Whatever may be the merits and the demerits of this volume, I earnestly trust that those who read and study it will realize that it certainly has been written through conviction. This chapter, however, is written only in the realm of opinion. In the world of art, as in the world of religion, there are many continents and islands, each one full of beauty, although varying. In painting there is the broad skill of the impressionist school, and the *finesse* of miniature art. There is the massive boldness of the oil-painting, and the delicate touch of the water-colour. In music, the same composition, whether vocal or instrumental, may have several interpretations, differing according to the mind of the executant, but each rendering may be good and thoroughly artistic. It will, therefore, be an advantage to the student to hear, as far as possible, the same music given by different performers, and then form an opinion as to which is the most effective rendering, and very probably he may take good points from each and incorporate them with his own ideas. A chat with friends, who are under different tuition from his own, may also bring good results to each party. The chief point for the singer is to bring a sense of earnestness and reality into the work. Mr. Hamilton Fyfe in the *Review of Reviews* (No. 375) says : ' The god of the art teacher is, in a word, technique.' If that be correct, then there must be very many bad art teachers. Technique is only the means whereby the end—that is, true art—can be attained.

' Nature is the art of God,' wrote Sir Thomas Browne, and surely it is the science of man gained by the study of nature which reveals to us ' the art of God.'

It is certainly so in Sinus Tone Production.

Science, that is technique, must as a study come first, but only because it is able to give the artist a power and freedom which he can obtain in no other way. Having become master of vocal science by the study of Nature, then is the artist able, with joy and wonder, more fully to appreciate and extensively use ' the art of God.'

The late Sir J. A. Thomson, in *Introduction to Science*, writes the following concise and very apt summary to his first chapter. ' The scientific mood,' he says, ' is especially marked by a passion for facts, by cautiousness of statement, by clearness of vision, and by a sense of the inter-relatedness of things. It is contrasted with the emotional or artistic mood, and with the practical mood, but the three form a trinity (of knowing, feeling, and doing) which should be unified in every normal life.'

Obviously, this was not written with any thought of the science of voice production, but ' Nature is an endless combination and repetition of a very few laws,'[1] and the suitability to vocal work of Sir Arthur Thomson's summary is only another instance ' of the inter-relatedness of things,' and a further proof that ' there are no watertight compartments in science.' The ' trinity of knowing, feeling and doing ' is indeed the vocal artist's complete outfit. One cannot over-estimate the importance of making ' knowing ' the first of the trinity. Unless that comes first it is in the highest degree improbable that the other two can follow. Know the machine which *creates* the tone. Know it in every detail and in every particular, and gain complete and absolute control over it. In that excellent and much-read book, *Interpretation in Song*, by Mr. Plunket Greene, the following statement is made on page 7 : ' Where the voice is *produced* goodness knows ; the singer certainly does not.' All honour and credit to Mr. Greene for the definite and straightforward admission. So far as we know, he is the only vocalist who has had the courage to own the fact that singers do not know where and how voice is produced. Surely such an admission from so eminent an authority is in itself at least one justification for the existence of the present volume. That the method of work herein expressed gives complete and satisfactory control of the vocal machinery can only be realized by those who have given it a thorough test and trial.

The second detail in the scientific trinity is *feeling*. This may

[1] J. P. Richter.

be translated as a clear comprehension as to the meaning of the author and composer in their writing, with a keen desire to express and present the sentiments to others—that is to say, to an audience. A simple illustration may be found in the well-known Somerset folk song, ' Oh, no John,' which is often given as a duet, but when taken as a solo, the vocalist should be most careful to portray the two characters, expressing the love and anxiety of John, and the feminine charm of the teasing coquette whom he admires. A study for the advanced singer is Schubert's ' Erl König.' Writing on this subject, Mr. Plunket Greene says : ' Here father, child and Erl King have to be clothed, staged and acted each in turn and each differently, while the horse and the wind are staged or heard in the accompaniment.' Again, in writing of the un-imaginative singer, he says: ' The rush of the wind and the gallop of the horse in the " Erl King " do not find him ready ; he is not shuddering with the father, shrinking with the child, or whispering with the " Erl King," . . . he is standing on the platform at Queen's Hall singing detached notes and phrases with great vocal ability.' But the reality and the intensity of the situation can be vividly depicted only when the *knowing*, the first of the trinity—in other words, technique—has been fully mastered. Thus, knowing + feeling = doing, that is the artist. A sign well known to most people is H_2O, which, being interpreted means, 2 parts of hydrogen + 1 part of oxygen = water. So we might well say, 2 parts of knowing + 1 part of feeling = the artist. The student will do well to remember the proportion that is given to knowing, for undoubtedly this is the part which demands the greatest time and patience.

A letter from Sir Edward Bairstow, of York Minster, dealing with vocalization appeared in the *Music Student* for February 1920. In it he states : ' Unless singing is expression and not mere tone production it is waste of time.' Clearly this statement cannot be contradicted. But the doctor continues : ' If it is a form of expression then it is a spiritual thing. It is no use trying to teach a spiritual thing as if it were entirely material. ' Here is the point where, in the author's opinion, hundreds go wrong with Sir Edward Bairstow. Singing is firstly a mechanical operation, just as mechanical as a pianola, governed by known scientific laws, and under the direct control of the artist. The student, having become master of the vocal machinery, is afterwards able to infuse his mind into the tone which he has learned to produce with the utmost ease, and then singing does indeed become a spiritual matter. Then is the trinity of knowing, feeling, and doing unified, and the scientist has become one with the glorious artist. The wise person will see to it that those two always walk hand in hand together throughout the artistic life. That which Necessity has joined together, Freedom may never put asunder. The marriage of the two must be indissoluble, without the possibility of any divorce.

Sir J. A. Thomson writes : 'It is certain, though rarely realized that science has precious gifts to place in the hands of art, that she may fashion them magically into beauty. Science has enormous treasure-caves full of what we cannot but describe as the raw materials of poetry. . . . It is beyond doubt that science, with its subtle revelations of the order of Nature, may enhance even the artist's visions.'

Here we have beautifully expressed the whole reason for the very existence of the present volume ; namely, that singing shall be brought into ' the order of Nature,' and not be degraded to the parrot-like condition of mere ' imitation.'

Let us then consider a few suggestions which may help the student to avoid some of the pitfalls that will surely be met in travelling the difficult and thorny pathway which leads to the promised land ; the land where the soul is not bound and fettered by mere speech because music has led it to the edge of the infinite.[1]

We have already urged the importance of actually personifying the character or characters who appear in the music. Of almost equal importance is advice given by Mr. Plunket Greene : ' Don't interpret where interpretation is not wanted.' Some might think such advice rather unnecessary, but experience has shown otherwise. A little time since, Schumann's ' Der Nussbaum ' was the selected song for the children's section in a musical festival competition. The adjudicator found fault with one of the small competitors because she did not ' act the song.' How a vocalist can be expected ' to act ' a nut tree is not very clear. In such a case we see the usefulness of Mr. Greene's advice. A song of this type requires merely smooth singing with a happy tone of voice, and certainly no action.

[1] The meaning of song goes deep. Who is there that in logical words can express the effect music has on us? A kind of inarticulate unfathomable speech which leads us to the edge of the infinite. CARLYLE.

A point of very great importance is the movement and position of the mouth. In the *Daily Telegraph* for 20th September 1919 it was stated in a letter signed ' Mus. Doc. Oxon.' that the author of this book, in his work, ' Science and Singing ' was the first to start a crusade against the universally accepted shibboleth of the open mouth. For many years it has been the continuous cry of every voice trainer to every pupil, ' Open the mouth,' and in some cases the poor student had to submit to the mouth being kept open with a cork between the teeth. The accompanying picture is a snapshot taken by a representative of the *Daily Mail* at a competitive musical festival in 1920. Such a gaping position of the mouth can hardly be considered graceful. But what of its utility ? A very small amount of consideration will show that the position is hopelessly wrong in every respect. Let the reader open his mouth wide, and in this position try to say the word ' feed.' It will at once be seen that the mouth must be closed in order to enunciate the word. If then the open mouth were a necessity it would be impossible to sing with even and equal tone, ' He shall feed His flock.' One knows, however, that the word ' feed ' can be sung with tone that is equally good as any other word in the sentence.

A little time since one of our best-known vocalists put as her initial item in a concert programme, ' Ocean, thou mighty monster ' (Weber).

With her mouth open to its utmost limit, she began: ' Ah-shun.'

Let the reader try to speak with a wide open mouth. Take such a simple phrase as ' Good morning, how are you ? ' If the mouth be opened *wide* for each separate word, the result will be ridiculous in the extreme. It is the adoption of the open mouth which has ruined the enunciation in song of so many vocalists. What we really want is a mouth capable of considerable variety in shape, and of very quick movement, so that the vowels shall not gradually slide into each other, but each one shall be kept pure and complete, until the next sound is ready to follow on. Bach once said : ' A scale ought to resemble a string of pearls, in which all the pearls are of equal size, and each touches the next without adhering to it.'

The idea is more intensely applicable to vowel sounds. When such work has had *real study* we shall not have any further articles on diction such as that which appeared in the *Daily Telegraph* for

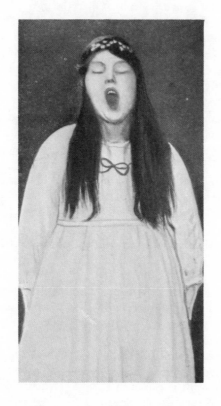

FIGURE 30. HER TOP NOTE !

27th August 1921. The author of the article styles himself ' Dum-Dum,' and, writing of an operatic performance he heard, says :

It was given me to hear the first remark and the first remark only that was uttered by the tenor. Each of the two basses opened his contribution with a gruff and cavernous ' bow-wow,' as if he were an enormous boar-hound. Having achieved this, he lapsed into an immobile mystery. From the ladies I took nothing, but my companion, keener of hearing than myself, did catch one statement, and that, by a miracle of luck, was a gem—' How irksome my weapon's weight.' After some two hours of majestic music, the great moment came, unexpectedly, as great moments should come. We were working through an immense duet, when one of the basses, stung apparently by the interminable persistence of his partner, was suddenly kindled to a momentary coherence. ' What demand'st thou ? ' he inquired sombrely. The lady he addressed, not in the least dismayed, seemed not unnaturally to take this as a challenge. Drawing herself up, she glared at him, and, with deliberate icy distinctness, enunciated, syllable by syllable, the remarkable reply : ' PHIR NAH KE PAH POO.' And the article ends ' What does it mean ? '

What, indeed !

On page 16 it was shown that breath coming from the vocal cords directly out of the mouth cannot possibly produce tone. Air activity must start in the head cavities. Now if the mouth be widely opened, the air is given every possible opportunity of escaping out of the mouth instead óf going into the sinuses. Keep the mouth fairly well closed and the breath is much more likely to take its proper passage into the head, and as a result produce vastly better tone. Mr. Plunket Greene gave much valuable assistance to the cause of vocalization in his excellent article on ' Economy in Diction,' which appeared in the *Daily Telegraph* for 6th September 1919. In that and subsequent issues of the *Daily Telegraph* and *Music Student*, he raised his powerful and very useful voice against what he termed ' jaw-wagging,' and without doubt many vocalists and tutors took the lesson to heart, with the result that the vigorously open mouth is now rather less in evidence, to the great advantage of all concerned.

An important detail, which very rarely has sufficient attention, is the matter of facial expression. Without wishing to encourage feminine—and probably one might include masculine—vanity, the mirror should be considered a valuable adjunct in vocal training. The *Strand Magazine* for June 1921 contains a very interesting article by Tetrazzini entitled ' My Life of Song,' and she makes the following excellent remarks : ' In the eyebrows alone you can depict mockery, every stage of anxiety and pain, astonishment, ecstasy, terror, suffering, fury, and admiration, besides all the subtle tones between. That is one reason why it is necessary to practise before the mirror to see that the correct facial expression is present.'

Some people are fortunate in being able to command with ease a very considerable variety of emotional expression. At one moment fun and good humour will ripple joyously over the whole face, and, in the twinkling of an eye, it will change to a demoniacal scowl which will make one shiver with fear. Very few people however possess this power as a gift; most students must work patiently and continually to get a thorough and easy command of facial expression, and should consider it a definite subject for study.

An obvious matter for consideration is where breath shall be taken in a song. Some people endeavour to sing too many notes with one breath. There are many cases in which it is distinctly advisable to take a second breath even though the music could be given with only one. An example of this is found in Albert Mallinson's charming song, ' Sing, break into song.'[1] (The publishers of the songs have very kindly given the author special permission to insert the following quotations.)

---

[1] Published by The Frederick Harris Co.

Very frequently this passage is taken in one breath because it is easy to do so, but the words gain an importance by taking a fresh breath for ' A song of the Blossoming May.' Another example of a similar kind is to be found in Cyril Scott's ' Lovely kind and Kindly loving.'[1]

If the phrase ' Sweet, fair, wise, kind, blessed, true ' be taken in one breath, it is much less impressive than if it be taken in two halves : ' Sweet, fair, wise—kind, blessed, true.'

Needless to say, there are plenty of musical phrases which demand much practice and considerable skill in order that the whole passage may be taken in one breath only. Their name is legion ; so there is no need to give special examples.

A point which is frequently missed by many amateurs and some professional singers, is the possibility of introducing a pause. If used with skill, either as a lengthened note, or as an absolute silence, an impressive and artistic effect may often be produced in this way. The vocalist however, should beware of making a frequent use of such means, as it will spell ruin to his success. It must be clearly understood that the pause must be considered

[1] Published by Elkin & Co.

as an essential part of the song, and not a break in it. Excellent examples of this can be heard in the gramophone records made by the late Gervase Elwes of Roger Quilter's ' O mistress mine ' and ' Blow, blow, thou winter wind.'[1] In the second verse of the former song—' What is love ? '—the crotchet for the word ' love ' is held on as though it were a dotted minim ; thus producing a very delightful artistic effect, besides giving more point to the question. A similar pause is made in the last line on the word ' mine.' In the song, ' Blow, blow thou winter wind,' a considerable lengthening of the quaver E produces a very happy result.

Then   heigh - ho   the hol - ly!

The Rev. Godfrey Thring's poem, ' Fierce raged the tempest o'er the deep,' set to music by the Rev. Dr. Dykes, is well suited in the last line to such treatment. The word ' Peace ' may with great advantage be considerably lengthened, and so give the idea of two separate commands, as intended by the author. First of all ' Peace,' then ' be still.' If taken in strict time the effect is that ' Peace ' is being told to ' be still,' making the word ' Peace ' a substantive, instead of a command. Many other instances could be given, both in hymns, psalms, and songs, where a lengthened note, an absolute silence, or a momentary change of time, could be used with telling effect to the listener. A certain church organist was resigning his office, and one of the choristers said sadly to him, ' Ah, Mr. Smith, we shall not get any of those beautiful pauses when you have gone.'

Let it be clearly understood that the pauses or changes *must be made* beautiful. They may be introduced only for a good and sufficient reason, and with a keen sense of balance, otherwise the

[1] Published by Boosey & Hawkes, Ltd.

thing of beauty becomes a matter of chaos as regards time and
absurdity as regards sentiment.

It may be well at this point to give a hint or two as to making
alterations in songs. As with the pause, such action requires
great judgment, and should never be attempted unless for very
excellent reasons, and then only providing it does not interfere
with the intention of the composer and with the spirit of the work.
The owners of the copyright of the undermentioned works have
very generously given me permission to use their songs as examples
of legitimate alteration.

We will take first Roger Quilter's delightful arrangement of the
old song, ' Drink to me only with thine eyes.'[1] It is usually
taken thus :

It would not be easy to improve Mr. Quilter's accompaniment,
but the sense of the words would be better conveyed by altering
the accent as follows :

and a similar alteration could be made at the end of the poem
' Not of itself but thee.'

The next example is taken from a very graceful song by
Dr. Arthur Somervell, ' On a summer morning.'[2]

[1] Published by Winthrop Rogers, Ltd
[2] Published by Boosey & Hawkes, Ltd.

The lark to Heav'n __ had borne my pain _____

It would be impossible in a song which bears evidence of such clever workmanship to make any serious improvement, but it seems to me that we get a better sense of triumph by altering the *finale* as suggested.

The lark to Heav'n __ had borne my pain _____

Another instance of a simple but, I think, valuable alteration can be found in a song which might well be in the repertoire of every soprano, namely, Mallinson's ' Snow-flakes.'[1] The song is distinctly a work of art, but I think it would gain effect by taking the last note on D an octave higher than written.

and it melts __ a - way!
und sie schmelzt so gleich! _____

[1] Published by The Frederick Harris Co.

There are times when it is advisable to omit a high note and use a low one. This is the case in an excellent but little-known song by Florence Vincent. The composer has set to interesting and very suitable music the well-known hymn by Mrs. Alexander, ' The roseate hues of early dawn.'[1] The *finale* is as follows :

Here it would be inartistic to take the word ' night ' on the upper G. There is nothing triumphant about the word 'night,' and the music comes to a more satisfying close by taking the downward rather than the upward movement. A vocalist choosing the top note would only do so with the obvious idea of showing off his high note, and this is the last thing any true artist would do. The last alteration which I would suggest here, is taken from the work of our clever contemporary, Frank Bridge, ' Go not, happy day,'[1] The work is melodious and original, and in my opinion could be improved by the alteration of one note only, that is, let G be substituted for C. This makes no alteration in the character of the music, and makes a valuable addition to the list of good tenor songs, by taking away a note which is too low for a tenor compass.

[1] Published by Winthrop Rogers, Ltd.

Fal - ters from her lips,

etc.

Perhaps the greatest gift next to voice which a singer can possess is the gift of a brilliant and vivid imagination. It is a qualification that gets too little attention. Sir Clifford Allbutt, in his presidential address to the British Medical Association at Cambridge in 1920, complained that even the universities do not build for the imagination as they used to do. To neglect what Coleridge once called ' the shaping spirit of imagination,' is to leave unused one of the most valuable assets that any artist can possess.

Imagination has been well termed ' the centre of creative life and action.' Sir Clifford Allbutt in the above-mentioned address insisted that science has need of imagination.

Indeed it has.

The scientist, providing he knows his work—acoustics, anatomy, etc.—can produce a good voice ; the composer may write a magnificent musical work ; but it requires the imagination of a combined Turner and Hans Andersen to unite the two elements and form a whole which pulsates with emotion and vibrant life. The most simple idea, the most slender and tiny subject, may be glorified and exalted into a matter of exquisite and radiant loveliness, providing the imaginative faculty has clothed it with grace, beauty, and reality. I remember once hearing a recitation at a public entertainment. The artist was Miss Ada Reeves, and never has any audience of 2,000 people been more completely spellbound for three minutes by means so utterly and wonderfully simple. Seated on a chair on the huge stage, she simply talked to an imaginary tiny son, Jim, in a cradle at her feet, whilst she plied an imaginary needle upon her handkerchief. No attempt was made for spectacular effect ; there was no music ; yet no picture could have been more vivid and real ; for everyone in that vast audience felt the intensity of the mother's pride and love for her darling Jim.

The speaker on the stage, with her brilliant imagination, was indeed 'the centre of creative life and action,' and everyone participated in the maternal joy of an affectionate parent devoted to her child.

Seeing that such a touching effect can be produced by mere speech, it is certain that the vocal artist, with the addition of music which should 'lead us to the edge of the infinite,' has a power which is even more telling and extended.

The *Morning Post*, in criticizing the first edition of this work (*Science and Singing*) spoke of it as 'a theory which requires for its acceptance a good deal more imagination than the ordinary individual is prepared to exercise'; and the prophecy has proved true. Yet the scientific imagination which produced that volume in 1909 has now penetrated the whole world. To the author's personal knowledge the system is being used in North and South America, in Australia, New Zealand and Africa, to say nothing of the continent of Europe. Clearly it was realized that vocal science was in need of an imagination greater 'than the ordinary individual is prepared to exercise,' but 'the ordinary individual' is the very one who will most profit by the long and often painful toil which brought together, and eventually pieced, in methodical and harmonious order, the varied and widely different facts which have made the Art of Sinus Tone Production a simple but scientific system.

This chapter would be incomplete unless mention was made of the necessity for perseverance in study, coupled with a high ideal.

Sink not in spirit. Who aimeth at the Sky
Shoots higher much than he who means a tree.

This should be the attitude of every worker in the world of music. It is true the arrow of our work may perhaps not reach to the sky of our ambition, but with a high aim it will travel far beyond the nearest privet hedge or laurel bush. Most workers in the art world have at some time felt the difficulty of keeping up a steady and unfalteringly high aim. One may work for so long, and produce such apparently small results. A source of inspiration may be found at such times in the flowing tide of the sea. I remember on one occasion standing on the cliffs at Margate wondering if the tide was on the ebb or flow. I saw that a wave had reached a certain point on the sand, for it had left its mark there, but from that point the water appeared to be receding.

L

I was not satisfied upon the point, and waited to make quite sure. I had to wait fifteen minutes before a wave came beyond the determining spot. For the whole of that fifteen minutes the tide appeared to be going back, but in reality it was coming up the whole time. Let the student remember that this is Nature's method of working. One may frequently work, and work, and work, and produce a result which seems to be almost *nil*, but providing the method is correct, the ultimate success need never be doubted, although it may be delayed. The wise student will not expect to find good results in a short time, but will bravely and perseveringly meet each difficulty, knowing that ' who aimeth at the sky ' has set himself a task that requires no small amount of energy and tact.

It is said that Rossini was once asked what was the chief qualification to make a good and successful vocalist. He replied : ' Voice.' Then said the questioner : ' What would you regard as the second qualification ? ' ' Voice,' said the great composer. ' Tell me, then, the third point that is necessary.' And again came the reply : ' Voice.'

The story may be very delightful to the person who has the God-given voice, for it leaves little necessity for real hard work. On the other hand, it gives but small hope to those musical enthusiasts who possess a keen love for music but little natural ability for singing it. To such, the ' trinity of knowing, feeling, and doing ' will be a new and joyful gospel, for it shall open to them ' the morning gate of the beautiful,' and they too shall enter the City of Song, and themselves have the wondrous happiness of joining in the glorious and immortal strains which the Divine God of Nature has with infinite love made possible to all those who know and follow His great and wonderful laws.

CHAPTER IX
SUMMARY

They are slaves who dare not be
In the right with two or three.—LOWELL.

THE TALE is told—the book is finished. We have, to the best of
our ability, put forward what we believe, and what experience has
shown to be, a simple, practical, and scientific method of voice
culture—a method which is void of contradictions and free from
anomalies, because it is based upon acoustic laws and anatomical
facts. It is a system which has been put to the severest tests, and
has not, so far, been found wanting.

The author is making no claim to finality. Far be it from him
to regard this work as the last word that can be said in the science
of voice production. Rather would he regard himself as a pioneer
in the matter, and although he may claim to be a leader in thought,
yet others will surely follow and show the possibility of further
developments and discoveries, based upon the labours and many
anxieties which have produced this volume.

No one would be so foolish as to say that in these days of
advancement and enlightenment we have discovered all that
human skill and ingenuity can ascertain. Who can say that nothing
now remains unconcealed ? The very existence of our Royal
Society in England, of the Académie des Sciences in Paris, and
of many kindred institutions throughout the world bears witness
to the fact that the man of science realizes that he has not yet
discovered all the laws which are unceasingly at work throughout
the universe ; neither may we consider that we have brought to
light all the facts which are laid up in the storehouse of the Eternal
God of Nature.

Singing is largely a matter of mind, and ' the mind does
not yet comprehend how it comprehends. Many things will
be cleared up when that surprising discovery is made,'[1] and
probably the full secret of the origin of speech and song will
not be known until we can fathom and explain what mind *is*,

[1] *Daily Telegraph*, 1st July 1920.

and elucidate the mystery why the material which we call 'brain' is able to hear sounds, see sounds, and feel the results of sound.

Aristotle was of opinion that the heart had its share of work in the production of tone, and he was, doubtless, right, for we have seen the nerve connection which exists between the vocal cords, the brain, and the heart. Yet how the brain and the heart influence that part of ourselves which forms the undying 'ego'—this we do not understand. But those who have devoted sufficient study to the matter do realize that the concentration of mind upon the sinuses in the way we have tried to describe, has a wonderful power in developing tone which is both beautiful and resonant. Here, at all events, is practical work, which another generation may possibly further develop.

Thus there is much work still to be done by the patient investigator and by the thoughtful worker.

O man, little hast thou learnt of truth in things most true;
How therefore shall thy blindness wot of truth in things most false ? [1]

Had Sir Isaac Newton lived to-day, instead of 240 years ago, he would still have likened himself to 'a boy playing on the sea-shore, and diverting himself in now and then finding a smoother pebble or a prettier shell than ordinary, while the great ocean of truth lay all undiscovered before him.'

An interesting endorsement of the correctness of his simile occurred six years after his death. The great philosopher had argued from his experiments that it would be quite impossible to design an achromatic lens, yet, in 1733, one was constructed by Chester Moor Hall.

A well-known writer has said : ' Let us beware of the loss of power to change our minds. The man who can never change his mind will never change anything outside it ; he will never be a cause again, except as an obstacle is a cause.' Let each one be careful not to act as an obstacle in the endeavour to fathom ' Nature '—' the word,' says Sir William Crookes, ' that stands for the baffling mysteries of the universe.'

Professor J. H. Poynting has well said : ' The hypotheses of science are continually changing. Old hypotheses break down and new ones take their place.' For many years Dalton's atomic theory was considered quite sound, but it has now given way to

[1] Tupper's *Proverbial Philosophy*.

the electron theory, and so we pass on from one page of Nature's 'infinite book of mystery' to another.

In *Nature* for 7th February 1907 Sir Michael Foster writes as follows : ' The science of physiology, as now understood, was scarcely recognized fifty years ago.' It is possible and probable, that during the next fifty years the art of singing will make equally great progress, for ' there is no stage in existence when we can say, " we are finished." The thing which we imagine we comprehend and understand to-day, may have to the awakened and ever-awakening mind a new meaning to-morrow, and will have still newer and newer interpretations in the future.'[1] Thus to the ' towering edifice of science new roofs and pinnacles and flying buttresses are added year by year, but the stones builded into the fabric by firm and skilful hands are not displaced.'

Some readers may feel inclined to smile at these thoughts, for experience has shown that in the department of vocal science some are unwilling to believe that there is much, or, indeed, anything, new that can be learned.

Singing, they argue, is a ' gift,' and no scientific ' fads ' of the present are likely to produce better singers than we have had in the past. So there the matter is left.

There are, however, others who would welcome a more definite and scientific method of vocal culture than that which is now in general use. They seem to realize that our present vocal theories, like 'Christianity and its traditional theology, have come down to us from an age very different from our own, an age when the sun and the stars moved round the earth, when the meaning of natural law . . . was only dimly apprehended.'[2] To such thinkers, this work has already made a very strong appeal, not only because of the straightforwardness of its theories, but still more on account of the practical results which have been gained.

Doubtless, there will be many who will feel some diffidence and hesitancy in throwing over the old vocal tenets and accepting a new creed.

' The imputation of novelty,' wrote John Locke, in a letter to the Earl of Pembroke in 1689, ' is a terrible charge amongst those . . . who can allow none to be right but the received doctrines. Truth scarce ever carried it by vote anywhere at its first

[1] *The Gift of Understanding*, by Prentice Mulford.
[2] *Foundations*.

appearance ; new opinions are always suspected, and usually opposed, without any other reason but because they are not already common. But truth, like gold, is not the less so for being newly brought out of the mine. It is trial and examination must give it price, and not any antique fashion.'

Let those, then, who are sincerely desirous of taking the right course in vocal training, give the matter a thorough ' trial and examination,' and think, first of all, of the various and numerous difficulties which have to be faced in accepting the orthodox vocal cord system.

For instance : *A*—How can half an inch of wet membranous tissue produce two octaves of sound ?

B—How, on scientific grounds, can an additional quarter of an inch of tissue produce sounds which are two octaves lower, when, according to all known acoustic laws, the additional length should be four times greater ? In other words, a soprano voice with half an inch of vocal cord sings as, roughly speaking, her lowest note. A bass, according to acoustic laws, should have vocal cords *two inches* in length to produce his lowest note, but his vocal cords are only three-quarters of an inch in length.

C—On what law do the vocal cords act when they keep the same pitch with a varying tension ?

D—What *satisfactory* reason can be given for the existence of the sphenoid sinus ?

E—How is it that people can speak and sing when not only the vocal cords, but even the whole of the larynx, has been cut out ?

Here are five important points for elucidation, and many more could be added. It is of no use for us to be like the ostrich, and hide our faces from these anomalies. They exist, whether we notice them or not, and, therefore, it is surely better to face them. But we have had these contradictions so long with us that we cease to notice them, and many have even learnt to regard them with love and reverence as part of the accepted state of things.

Unless these questions can be definitely and conclusively settled, we shall certainly be straining at the gnat of Sinus Tone Production, whilst we willingly swallow the camel of vocal cord production. How frequently has the camel of familiar error been complacently accepted, whilst the gnat of a more or less imaginary difficulty has given untold trouble. But, surely, fifty gnats are more easily dealt with than one obstinate camel.

One gnat which has caused trouble to a good many people is the fact that we have had glorious singers in the past, when 'faddists' were unknown, and it is in the highest degree improbable that such singers as Grisi, Mario, Lablache, and others can ever be surpassed.

This is quite true, and we make no claim that our system will produce better singers than Jenny Lind and artists of a similar type.

A very illuminating and interesting sidelight upon Jenny Lind is given by Liza Lehmann in her excellent work, *Practical Hints for Students of Singing*.[1] Therein she states :

One of the secrets of successful placement and preservation of the voice is, I am yearly more and more convinced . . . the proper use of the ' head voice,' and the capacity to use it throughout the whole compass. I had the great privilege when a young girl of being allowed to attend the lessons given at her own house by the great Jenny Lind to her pupils from the Royal College of Music. She had then long retired from her absolutely unique career, and although a woman of advanced years, she would illustrate with her own still phenomenal voice many marvellous vocal effects, and one which I particularly remember was the power of using ' head voice ' throughout her entire compass, even to its lowest notes. . . . At the risk of repetition, I contend, in the light of accumulated experience, that this capacity to use head tones everywhere brings health to the voice and preserves it . . . . I have proved the helpfulness of this again and again by passing on the hint to singers who have come to rehearse with me, and who have benefited in a most marked manner.

Surely we have here in a nut shell the whole essence of this book, namely, ' the power of using the head voice throughout the entire compass.' Madame Liza Lehmann expressly states in her book that she intends to give merely ' practical hints.' *Science and Singing* puts the whole idea upon a scientific basis, from which the vocalist can gain absolute control over the vocal machine. Moreover, a reasoning and intelligent system must of necessity be of greater value and use than a mere blind obedience to advice, no matter how good that advice may be. There is no doubt that hundreds of singers, both directly and indirectly, have benefited by the advice which has thus been handed down from Jenny Lind. This book puts the advice upon an anatomical and scientific foundation, although, so far, none of our colleges, either musical

[1] Published by Enoch & Sons, London.

or medical, has officially recognized the fact.[1] If, however, our book-shelves could speak there are hundreds which could testify how valuable has been the addition of this volume to the library. When the system has become universal we may probably have a larger proportion of singers of a quality equal to although not better than, Jenny Lind. At present, however, it must be owned that the world sees very few vocalists of this standard.

Professor Sir J. A. Thomson wrote: ' It is certain that letting the mind play among facts has often led to magnificent conclusions. It seems that the solution is often reached first, and the proof supplied afterwards.' Probably this remark was intended to apply to the working of one individual mind. It is, however, equally true, and more applicable here with reference to two individuals. More than seventy years ago Jenny Lind realized that all vocal tone can be produced in the head. The *how* and the *why* she did not know and probably did not care. The knowledge answered her purpose, both for herself and pupils. Again quoting Professor Thomson: '*The system works*, therefore the unseen bridge across the gap must be there.' In 1847 Jenny Lind first appeared in London with extraordinary success, using a certain system of voice production which produced marvellous practical results. In 1909 *Science and Singing* was published, and the world had an opportunity of knowing *why* Jenny Lind produced such wonderful tone, although at that time the author was unaware that he was following theoretically the great singer's practical system. Messrs. Burroughs, Wellcome & Co., the well-known chemists, give an interesting example of practice preceding theory in a ' Lecture Memoranda Book' issued for the British Medical Association in 1910. The information is as follows :

Referring to the advent of aseptic surgery, an amusing story is told of a veterinary surgeon in Yorkshire, who practised over a century ago, and was famed throughout the countryside as a most successful operator. When asked as to his method of treatment, he always evaded the question with great astuteness, and would never give away the secret of his success. At length, when he grew to be a very old man, and became

[1] In February 1937 I was engaged to give a lecture on Sinus Tone Production to the authorities and students at the Convent of the Sacred Heart, W.10. This was such a success that I was asked to give some individual lessons and the system is now recognized and taught at the college to the 110 students who are there training for the scholastic profession. Since then the St. Augustine's Abbey School, Ramsgate, has adopted the system.

bowed down with age, and weight of years, he was again implored by his son to tell him, before he died, what he did in the secret half-hour that he always gave himself before operating. Life was ebbing, when the old man at length whispered, with his passing breath into his son's ear, ' I biles my tools.'

Thus elementary antiseptic work was practised years before Lord Lister's genius placed it upon a definite system. The details of his glorious success are now a matter of history. Sinus Tone Production has its history in the future, and other writers will one day pen a record of its fortunes.

Writing in the *Daily Telegraph* of Saturday 18th April 1914 upon ' Coming Opera,' Mr. Robin H. Legge, the well-known musical critic, says : ' But precisely why the greater schools [of music] produce so few potential opera singers, I fail to understand.' Backed up by Government and municipal assistance, to say nothing of private generosity, these schools attract the best talent to be found in the kingdom, so that they certainly possess every possible opportunity. Moreover, the very few really fine vocalists who do appear out of the thousands who are trained, are invariably endowed by Nature with such special and peculiar gifts, that the wondrous charm of their magic voice is quite as much the result of inborn ability as the result of any system in training.

This fact is made quite evident in studying the lives of many of our best artists. Alboni saw Adelina Patti when she was only six years old, and was so impressed with her voice that she immediately foretold a very great future for her. At the age of seven she made her first public appearance in New York, and thereafter would never consent as a child to go on to the stage without a doll. In the *Musical Times* for July 1921 the well-known musical critic, F.E.B., remarks, ' Patti owed everything to Nature and nothing to art.' Madame Albani admitted that although she learnt style and phrasing from the great master Lamperti, yet her voice was ' Nature's own gift.' Again, quoting from the article by Tetrazzini in the *Strand Magazine* for April 1921, it is stated that when a child of ten she applied to the Florence Conservatoire for entrance as a student, the Principal in astonishment exclaimed, ' If she can sing like this why does she come here at all—is it *to teach us* ? ' Again, Mozart and his sister touring as pianists through Europe when they were quite children are good examples of a special musical talent, quite apart from training ; whilst the marvellous boy-conductor, Willy Ferrero, who at seven and a half years of age was complete master of an orchestra of ninety performers, whom he directed entirely from memory, shows that Dame Nature is still prodigal in her free gifts to the few.

These very clever performers, however, seldom make the best teachers. Their exclusive powers have come to them without very serious self-denial or perseverance ; and therefore they are unable to appreciate the difficulties encountered by the ordinary or less gifted student.

A well-known writer[1] has truly said that ' the public are served not by what the Lord Mayor feels, who rides in his coach, but by what the apprentice boy feels, who looks at him.'

One of the practical advantages claimed for Sinus Tone Production is that the apprentice boy—that is to say, *anyone*, no matter how unmusical—can on these lines be taught to sing well ; whilst those who already sing well can, with very few exceptions, be taught to sing very much better. The tone which can be produced is generally sweeter and more powerful. It is, in fact, similar to the tone which the vocal genius produces, without knowing exactly *how* it is done.

Other worrying gnats can be dealt with in an equally simple manner by the trained mind.

It is an undoubted fact that, although truth is very, very hard to find, yet, when found, it is often harder still to get it recognized. Probably one reason for this may be found in the fact that the cult of the bigot is always in our midst, and must be reckoned with as a restraining factor in the march of progress ; for the truth of the parallel expressed by Thomas Moore has often been proved, namely, that ' the mind of the bigot is like the pupil of the eye, the more light you throw upon it, the more it contracts.' To people of this type, any appeal outside their own narrow sphere is quite useless.

John Locke, in his famous *Essay on the Human Understanding*, deals with this point in a manner which has a considerable bearing upon the subject which we have in hand. He is writing, in Chapter XXXIII, upon ' The Association of Ideas,' and says :

Some of our ideas have a natural correspondence and connection with one another ; it is the office and excellency of our reason to trace these, and hold them together in that union and correspondence which is founded in their peculiar beings.

Besides this there is another connection of ideas wholly owing to

[1] Colton.

chance or custom : ideas that in themselves are not at all of kin, come to be so united in some men's minds that it is very hard to separate them ; they always keep in company, and the one no sooner at any time comes into the understanding, but its associate appears with it. . . . Some independent ideas, of no alliance to one another, are, by education, custom, and the constant din of their party so coupled in their minds that they always appear there together, and they can no more separate them in their thoughts than if they were but one idea, and they operate as if they were so. This gives sense to jargon, demonstration to absurdities, and consistency to nonsense ; . . . it makes men incapable of conviction, and they applaud themselves as zealous champions for truth, when, indeed, they are contending for error.[1]

How wonderfully these words coincide with what has taken place, and is still happening, when the teachings of ' Science and Singing ' are discussed. One can never mention the word *voice*, but the vocal cords and the larynx at once come into the mind. People can indeed ' no more separate them in their thoughts, than if they were but one idea, and they operate as if they were so.'

I fully realize that many of those who are loudest in the denunciation of the new theory, do ' applaud themselves as zealous champions for truth,' notwithstanding the fact that, unwittingly, ' indeed they are contending for error.' It is the fate of pioneers to become the targets of sceptics. But if these sceptics and ' defenders of the faith ' be really ' zealous champions for truth,' it is only reasonable to suppose that they will have good and weighty reasons to give for the cause which they so strenuously uphold, and for the faith that is in them. We will therefore ask one of these pillars of orthodoxy, 'On what grounds do you believe that the vocal cords create tone, and what proof have you that they do so ? ' An answer given by one of our prominent public singers was, ' I can *feel* the vocal cords vibrate when I sing,' and the gentleman considered this was an all-sufficient proof of the matter. But ' If science is to be consistent, it has to set itself to the task of distinguishing realities from appearances.'[2]

In the *Musical Standard* for 23rd April 1910 appeared a letter over the initials ' F.H.K.,' in which the writer shows himself quite incapable ' of distinguishing realities from appearances,' and exhibits an utter ignorance of even elementary acoustics. In a letter not over burdened with good taste he states, all in capital letters, in order to impress the reader with the importance and the

[1] See Appendix M, page 170.
[2] *Introduction to Science* by the late Prof. J. A. Thomson.

truth of the fact, ' VIBRATION IS SOUND.' As well might
one say, ' Sailors are admirals,' ' Wood is doors,' or ' Fruit is
apples.' *Sound* is vibration, undoubtedly, and it is quite impossible
to have sound without it, but vibration, besides being sound,
is also light, colour, electricity[1] ; and, it may be, as in the case of
the vocal cords, a mere movement and nothing more. A steel
bridge vibrates as a train passes along it, one's house may vibrate,
the hand may vibrate, but in none of these cases is sound produced. Thus, neither the sensation of vibration in the larynx nor
the laryngoscopic perception of movement conveys the slightest
proof of the sonority of the vocal cords. A red Indian or anyone
else who saw a locomotive for the first time, might well think that
the coupling rod which connects the two driving wheels was the
cause of the train's movement, for the simple reason that the train
never starts until the coupling rod moves. Such an idea would
of course be an utter absurdity to an engineer, but it is on the same
plane as the assumption that the vocal cords create tone because
we see or feel them move.

Another so-called ' proof ' that the throat is the centre of vocal
sound, is the fact that when the throat is affected by cold or sore-
ness the power of song is at once impaired. Here again, we have
a difficulty which appears as a mountain to many minds, but in
reality is only a mole-hill that can be easily removed. The larynx
is a part, and an important part, of the means whereby tone is
created. The title-page of this book will show that this fact has
not been overlooked, for it is there stated that the volume is ' A
consideration of the capabilities of the vocal cords and *their work*
in the art of tone production.' Now it is quite evident that any
piece of machinery, be it large or small, may be rendered useless
by a loose bolt, a bent pin, or any such simple cause. We should
therefore, in any case, expect that the failure of the vocal cords to
do their share of work in a satisfactory manner would have a
detrimental effect upon the voice. It was many years ago that
the people of Corinth were reminded, ' That there should be no
schism in the body, . . . and whether one member suffer, all the
members suffer with it.' A violent headache, or a severe nervous
strain, may impair singing quite as much as a sore throat does.
It is, however, a fact of no small importance that the person who
understands the art of Sinus Tone Production is not inconvenienced

[1] See page 107.

by throat troubles to one-half, or even one-quarter, the extent of the one who knows nothing or little of the system. A notable instance of this is given on page 15. The whole of the five months that the patient was attending hospital she had the power of speech, but was unaware of the fact. She only became conscious of her power after having two lessons in Sinus Tone Production. It must, therefore, be emphatically urged that because a person has a sore throat or a damaged larynx which interferes with the voice, this cannot be accepted as proof that the individual is really unable to sing ; it only shows that under existing conditions he does not know how to do so. The truth of this has been demonstrated many times. So ' proof ' number two disappears.

Some people might argue that a system which is so ancient, and has permitted such an array of magnificent singers in the past and present to pursue their calling, and enthral the world of song with glorious tone, should be good enough for our children. Part of the reply to that argument has already been given on page 154, but let it be remembered that there is another and a very serious side to the question. The system of vocal cord tone production is *entirely* responsible for all the stammering with which we meet, and also for the whole of that trouble known as ' clergyman's sore throat.' Besides the heavy weight of these two evils, it must. also take a very large share in the creation of ' nodes,' inflammation, laryngitis, etc. Therefore, the argument of the good it has permitted is heavily overbalanced by the evils it has created. Thus, whatever opinions may be formed as to the merits or demerits of Sinus Tone Production, it would appear on examination to be fairly evident that the foundations upon which the vocal cord system is built are of an unstable and very weak character. No wonder that the worshippers of this Diana are anxious as to the safety of her temple. We have already cited many instances from the time of Athanasius, A.D. 326, to that of Lord Lister, A.D. 1872, where men, having distinctive ideas, have been laughed to scorn by their contemporaries. Yet, in each case, posterity sees how blind were the authorities who attempted to extinguish the new light.

Many more instances could be mentioned, but one other will suffice. It is an important one, because of the very high position which the objector held in the world of science. We refer to Michael Faraday, who looked upon the possibility of getting ' electric light ' as nothing less than ridiculous. What would he say if he could see the thousand and one uses to which electricity is now put ?

There are many who have thought it right to look upon these vocal theories with pity and contempt. In the light of history, this must be expected. It has been said that ' Nature sells her secrets at a price,' and contempt and ridicule are part of the price.

Frequently, though happily not always, the principal meed of thanks which is offered to the discoverer is a public statue after his death ; not a great reward, surely, for the years of toil and hard grind inevitably exacted by all original thought of any real value.

The leader on ' The Reward of Research ' in the *Daily Telegraph* for 3rd March 1920[1] points out that ' some of the greatest names in the history of British science are associated with melancholy stories of struggle continued over many years. For such triumphs are not achieved without the devotion of a great part of a man's life. Koch's discovery of the tubercle bacillus was the fruit of eleven years of patient seeking.' This volume is the result of fifteen years ' of patient seeking '![2]

Still, there is no small satisfaction in feeling that one has been able to add some knowledge, be the amount ever so small, to the lore of the world, which shall be of distinct advantage to one's fellow creatures for all time.

Here the matter must be left.

The author has spared neither time nor pains in the sincere effort to rescue our beloved art from the undignified and un-satisfactory position of being the only art which depends for its success chiefly upon mere imitation.

'By unremitting work—the solvent of most difficulties'[3]—he has tried to show—as far as mere writing can show—that a voice may be built upon acoustic laws, which entirely coincide with the anatomy of the vocal machine, when it is regarded simply as a wind instrument, without the addition of any reed.

It must rest entirely with the readers of this volume whether the work shall have a success commensurate with the amount of labour and time which has been expended upon it.

[1] See page 54.

[2] This was written in 1922. Now in January 1938, another fifteen years ' of patient seeking' have been added, the results of which will be found in *Sinus Tone Production*. Published by J. M. Dent & Sons Ltd. Price 7/6.

[3] Taken from the address of Sir William Crookes, F.R.S., V.P.C.S., before the British Association, at Bristol, 1898.

Many musicians, both professional and amateur, have already expressed in no uncertain manner their appreciation of the benefits they have received by working upon the methods here indicated.

If the future brings as much success in proportion as the past has done, the system will very soon be outside the range of those who fire at it as ' a mere fad.' If the work be untrue, their shots will soon sink it, but if true, all the shots and all the opposition in the world will never stop its progress.[1] The author has quite sufficient confidence in it to make him quite willing to await events, the while echoing Carlyle's sentiments : ' May Time, which solves or suppresses all problems, throw glad light on this also.'[2]

If, however, the book is to take a permanent place in the libraries of the musicians of the present and of future generations, it will be because those who have put its theories to a proper test realize to some extent the labour which has been entailed in writing it ; they will also value and proclaim the benefits they have themselves received in studying the system of Sinus Tone Production.

Lastly we would point out how these ideas and plans bring into harmony the conflicting convictions of theorists in the art of singing and of those who practise it.

Dr. Aikin, in his book, *The Voice*,[3] says :

Everyone who approaches the subject of voice production is amazed and perplexed at the extraordinary diversity of opinion which exists among those who are to be regarded as authorities in the matter. . . . There can be no doubt that the deficiency of scientific facts which can be clearly demonstrated, is at the root of the lamentable confusion of ideas in connection with the voice.

Yet it is evident that Dr. Aikin himself is in direct opposition to some of his own brethren, for we have seen that he himself points out that *sixteen times* more exertion and air pressure are required for a high note than for a low one ; whilst Dr. Latson, with equal truth theoretically, and more truth practically, says : ' Any muscular action of the throat will impair—may absolutely ruin—the tone.'

The theorist declares that a knowledge of the structural mechanism of the vocal apparatus must be of practical use and value to the singer, therefore he must certainly study its anatomy. Undoubtedly, too, the argument—as an argument—is correct.

---

[1] This fifth edition of the work shows the statement to be true.
[2] *Sartor Resartus.*
[3] Original edition, published by The Macmillan Company, London.

The engine driver must understand every bolt and hinge in his locomotive ; the architect must know the smallest detail of the building he is superintending ; and it is of great value to the pianist to know something both of the mechanism of his instrument, of acoustic laws, and of the muscles which control the hand and arm. Against this, the successful practical singer says, ' It is not the slightest help to me in singing to know anything whatever about the details of my throat ; in fact, the less I think about them the better do I sing.' Not a few of the best teachers are also of the same mind.

Thus, the opinions of the theorists and the practice of the vocalist are at variance, and neither can convince the other that his opinions are wrong.

As a matter of fact, each one is, to a certain extent, right. A study of anatomy is of the greatest practical help to the singer. It gives him the knowledge whereby he can produce a bigger volume of tone as well as a better quality. But it is the anatomy of the head that demands attention, not the muscles of the throat. The first lesson in vocalization should always be prefaced by a study of the anatomy of the head, and a clear comprehension of its structure should be in the pupil's mind before a commencement is made in practical work. Then will theory and practice be found to go hand in hand. ' Science and Singing ' will no longer clash with discordant sounds, and aching throats will not testify to the reality of the quarrel, but delightful ease—delightful both to the listener and the singer—coupled with brilliant tone—will bear ample evidence of the wonderful results that can be obtained when practice and theory in harmony unite to form ' The Voice Beautiful.'

I can think of no words which will more suitably close this volume than the final passage in Lord Lister's introductory lecture at King's College, delivered on the afternoon of 1st October 1877 : ' And thus I believe that we have taken one sure step in the way of removing this important but most difficult question from the region of vague speculation and loose statement into the domain of precise and definite knowledge.'

APPENDICES

M

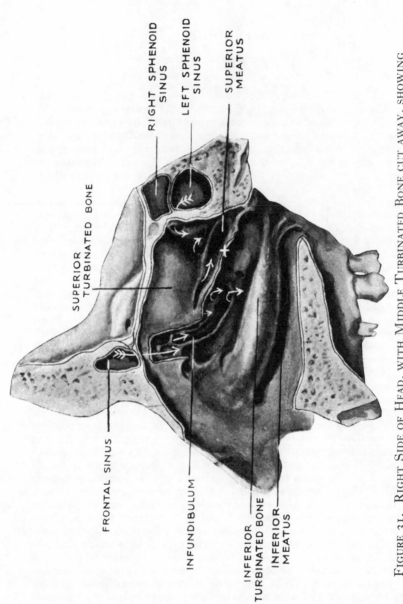

RIGHT SPHENOID SINUS

LEFT SPHENOID SINUS

SUPERIOR MEATUS

SUPERIOR TURBINATED BONE

FRONTAL SINUS

INFUNDIBULUM

INFERIOR TURBINATED BONE

INFERIOR MEATUS

FIGURE 31. RIGHT SIDE OF HEAD, WITH MIDDLE TURBINATED BONE CUT AWAY, SHOWING INFUNDIBULUM

APPENDICES

A, PAGE 27

The study of Figure 31, like all matter under the heading of Appendices, is not a really essential point. It has, however, an indirect bearing upon the subject and will certainly be found interesting. The first point to notice is that in this specimen the sphenoid sinus on the right side is not on the same level as that on the left. Moreover the left sinus has crossed beyond the line of the centre and penetrated the right side of the head. The frontal sinus is very small.

Along the line at + the middle turbinated bone has been cut away in order to show the infundibulum behind it. The air in the frontal sinus does not in this case make its exit by way of the infundibulum, but in front of it, directly into the middle meatus. If the reader will very carefully and thoughtfully compare this figure with those between pages 16 and 17, and between 26 and 27, it will be seen what infinite variety is possible, and exists, in the formation of the bones which lie between the hard palate of the mouth and the roof of the nasal cavity. That there should be variety in voices under such conditions is only what we should expect. How different is it on the vocal cord theory, when the closest examination fails to give any indication whatever of either quality or pitch in voice. After the accumulated experience of many years, it is still impossible even to tell the difference between the cords of a tenor and a bass, or between a soprano and a contralto. To all appearances, they are exactly the same, and doubtless are so, for as 'Breath Governors' (see page 53) there is no reason why they should vary. In the *Music Student* for July 1920, Sir Edward Bairstow writes : ' To read many of the books on Singing, one would think . . . that the study of nasty pictures of your inside and the memorizing of crack-jaw names was the one remedy for all faults.' Personally speaking, I hold a very high opinion of Sir Edward ; and I trust he will not include these as ' nasty pictures.' It seems to me they illustrate a very wonderful and beautifully delicate instrument, and I hope our musical authority at York Minster will agree with me that the term ' beautiful ' is more applicable to these particular pictures than ' nasty.' With respect to ' memorizing crack-jaw names,' no such necessity exists in this work. Occasionally a long name is used to indicate a certain detail, but in such a case one is compelled to use the word, because there is no other whereby the fact can be stated. There is no need in any case to memorize even one ' crack-jaw word.' With respect to the terms frontal sinus, ethmoid cells, and sphenoid sinus, the cavities which are so known in the medical world could be known equally well to the singer as positions one, two, and three, or A, B, and C, and this should be made clear to every vocal student. The whole point is, that their relative positions must be known, in order to get the voice under full control. The names, ' crack-jaw ' or otherwise, do not matter one jot.

B, PAGE 38

' Nature abhors a vacuum.' For the benefit of the uninitiated, it might be well to explain that this means, that there cannot be anywhere an empty space unless very special means—such as an air pump—are taken to produce a vacuum. For instance if one takes a glass of water and empties the fluid away, air fills the glass as fast as the water goes out ; in just the same way as when one puts a finger in a glass of water, and then gradually withdraws the finger, there is no gap left in the water as the finger is withdrawn, but the fluid takes the place of the finger. So when the breath is started downwards from the points XN, XD, Figure 3, the remainder of the breath from the lungs upward is compelled to follow of its own accord, and that without any *driving* power. The same action takes place in emptying a vessel of fluid by means of a siphon. Although quite irrelevant to the matter under consideration, it is distinctly interesting to note that the fact that ' Nature abhors a vacuum ' is only true in a limited sense. The air which we breathe reaches, roughly speaking, to a height of about 170 miles above us. This 170 miles of air exerts a pressure of about fourteen pounds to the square inch, and so prevents the existence of any natural vacuum on this globe of ours. Beyond that 170 miles, however, a huge vacuum exists, greater than the mind of man can calculate.

C, PAGE 39

It is perhaps well to mention that allusion is here made simply to the practice of technical exercises. In the *Music Student* for May 1914, is an excellent article by Walter Ford, ' On Learning to Sing.' Therein the writer states : ' Will the result, not the process.' Here is advice which apparently is in direct opposition to mine. But it would appear from the context of Mr. Ford's article, that he is referring to method in the delivery of a song, and not in the study of technique. If that be so, I entirely agree with him, and there is nothing contradictory in the two opinions.

D, PAGE 53

In a lecture by Mr. Hubert Bath, A.R.C.M., before the Incorporated Society of Musicians, on Saturday, 14th March 1914, upon ' Kaffir War-dances and Modern Music,' a most interesting example was given of a very definite family likeness which exists between a Scotch melody—' A Churning Song,' which is to be found in Mrs. Kennedy-Fraser's charming volume, ' Songs of the Hebrides ' (Boosey & Co.) —and a Hindoo melody from Kashmir. By very kind permission of Mrs. Kennedy-Fraser and of Mr. Hubert Bath, the two melodies are here reproduced, and will endorse the scepticism expressed by the well-known musical critic, Mr. Robin H. Legge, as to the existence of so-called 'nationality' in music.[1]

A CHURNING SONG

HINDOO MELODY

E PAGE 55

It gives the author great pleasure to acknowledge here the great moral help and encouragement which he has received by studying the *Life of Lord Lister*, by Guy T. Wrench, M.D. (London), The book should, if possible, have a place in every home, giving as it does a brilliant example to the young man who is entering the difficulties of life, much encouragement to the man of middle age who is in the midst of them, and a whole mine of interest to young and old who have even a spark of enthusiasm for those who contend for right and truth against heavy odds. The fact that the book was written by a medical man of distinction, gives the volume much added authority and value, and the author of *Science and Singing* is deeply grateful to Dr. Wrench for the manly and straightforward way in which the facts of Lord Lister's life are given.

To one who is engaged in a heavy struggle for what he is convinced is the truth, it is no small encouragement to know that Dr. Lister was nine years in Glasgow effecting cures in a manner which had never before been known in the history of the world. At the end of the nine years he left for Edinburgh, but the medical men of his city 'for the most part failed to recognize him.' Surely, what a failure for them! It was seven years before Lister's discovery was even tried in London, during which time he had 'won the leading surgeons of Germany and France to his side,' and then London declared it to be a failure. It was 'a return to the dark days of surgery,' it was a 'carbolic mania,' etc. Yet he 'continued quietly with his work, knowing full well that it was of such a character as would eventually force the profession to follow his dictation.' It is true that the profession did '*eventually* follow his dictation,' but Denmark, Germany, and France all took precedence

[1] See *Daily Telegraph*, 19th May 1917.

of London in doing so. In Germany, Lister was treated as a hero, whilst London was sneering at him. Scotland and the Continent had known and fully appreciated the incomparable value of antiseptic treatment for twelve years before London surgeons as a body acknowledged its benefits. Still, we may thank Heaven, Lister did conquer, and that in a noble and gentlemanly manner. At a banquet given to him by the leading scientists of France, Dr. Pinard ended his speech by saying : ' Lord Lister, when we are asked why you are illustrious, we reply, because you have driven back death itself ; because in all you have done you have only caused tears of joy and gratitude.' What a truly beautiful phrase is the last one, and how few people there are of whom such a statement could be made ! Two years later, when he was seventy-five years of age, the Royal Society gave a banquet in his honour. Mr. Bayard, the American Ambassador, was present, and in the course of his speech said : ' My Lord, it is not a profession, it is not a nation, it is humanity itself, which with uncovered head salutes you.'

But let it ever be remembered that Horatius,

'. . . who kept the bridge so well
In the brave days of old,'

displayed no more courage in dealing with the enemies of Rome, than did Lister in his long fight year after year against the shortsightedness, the ignorance and the jealousy of an orthodoxy which hated a system that was better than its own.

F, PAGE 57

Another very interesting point which may be noticed (although it has no direct bearing upon the matter we are considering) is the fact that above and below the cords, the epithelium (that is, the outside skin) is what is known as ciliated. That is to say, from ten to twenty flattened blade- or hair-like appendages, about the 3,000th part of an inch in length, grow on each individual cell which forms the skin or epithelium. The particular work of these cilia is to carry outwards along the trachea, towards the mouth, the mucus formed by the mucous glands in these regions. The epithelium, however, which covers the cords themselves, is not ciliated, but stratified. The nails growing upon our finger-tips are one variety of this stratified or pavement epithelium. This kind of skin, being firmer and harder than the ciliated, gives the cords much added strength, and being also non-cellular, the breath can pass along easily and smoothly. The alteration of the epithelium in this particular spot is a most wonderful provision of Nature for the strengthening and assistance of vocal work.

G, PAGE 88

Claudius Galenus was son of Nicon, an architect of eminence. He was born at Pergamus, in Mysia and died in Sicily. With intense earnestness he devoted himself to the study of philosophy, mathematics, physic,

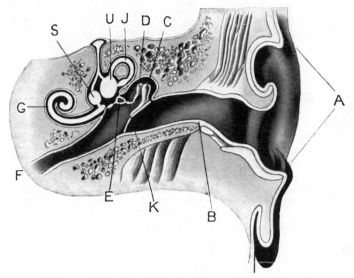

FIGURE 32. DIAGRAM OF EAR
An explanation of the Key letters appears on opposite page.

and anatomy. As a medical man he was so successful that some attributed his extraordinary cures to magical art. He himself attributed much of his success to the writings of Hippocrates. His diligence and industry must have been astonishing, for he wrote no less than 200 volumes. In many matters his reasoning has been found false, and his opinions ill-grounded. That being so, it is curious that his vocal theories should have stood until the present day.

H, PAGE 100

' Arachnoid.' The brain and the spinal cord are enclosed by three separate and distinct membranes. The innermost is technically known as the *pia mater* and the outermost as the *dura mater*. The arachnoid is a very thin and remarkably delicate and transparent membrane, which comes between the two.

J, PAGE 104

For the purpose of medical study, the ear, that is to say, the whole of the auditory organ, is divided into three sections, named respectively, the external, the middle, and the internal ear. The external ear—or we might well call it the external *part* of the ear—consists of the auricula and the external acoustic meatus. The auricula—denoted by the lines *A* in Figure 32[1]—is attached to and projects from the side of the head. The line at *B* points to the external acoustic meatus ; that is the passage which leads to the ear-drum or tympanic membrane.

The middle ear comprises the auditory tube—frequently known as the Eustachian tube—marked *F*, together with three bones which cross it, and connect the tympanic membrane, *K*, with the internal ear. The auditory tube leads to the nasal part of the pharynx, and is in communication with the mouth. It is by means of this tube that an equal pressure of air is maintained on the two sides of the ear-drum. The three bones at the upper end of the tube are known as the malleus or hammer bone (*C*), the incus or anvil bone (*D*), and the stapes or stirrup bone (*E*). The malleus is the largest of these three bones, and it will be noticed that one part of it is connected with the tympanic membrane. This part of the malleus is technically known as the manubrium, or handle of the malleus. It is fixed directly on to a layer of cartilage, and the cartilage is fixed to the ear-drum. The cartilage and ear-drum are seen at *K*. The malleus (*C*) works the incus (*D*), and the incus works the stapes (*E*), which fits into a portion of the internal ear.

The internal ear, or osseous labyrinth, consists mainly of three sections—the cochlea at one end (*G*), so named because of its spiral and shell-like appearance, the three semi-circular canals (*J*) at the other end, with a chamber known as the vestibule coming between and connecting the two. In the drawing, the base of the stapes is seen

[1] Taken from *Cunningham's Text Book of Anatomy*.

fitting into an opening in the bony wall of the vestibule, which opening is known as the fenestra vestibuli.

S and *U* are two membranous sacs enclosed within the vestibule, named respectively the saccule and the utricle.

Figure 32 gives an excellent idea of the external and middle sections of the ear, but the inner section will be better understood if compared with Figure 33, which is taken by special permission of Sir Ed. Schafer, D.Sc., F.R.S., from his *Text Book of Microscopic Anatomy*. The title given to this drawing by Sir Ed. Schafer is ' Plan of the Membranous Labyrinth, showing by shading the places where the nerve fibres are distributed.'

FIGURE 33.   PLAN OF THE MEMBRANOUS LABYRINTH

This membranous labyrinth is enclosed within the osseous or bony labyrinth, and inasmuch as the shape of the two is practically identical, it seemed to me that this drawing (Figure 33) would give an excellent idea of the shape and ramifications of the internal ear, with the additional advantage of ' showing by shading the places where the nerve fibres are distributed.'   In Figure 32 it is possible to show only one of the semi-circular canals.   Figure 33 gives an excellent plan of the three. The membranous labyrinth contains a fluid termed endolymph, which is free to flow to all parts, as the three semi-circular canals, the vestibule, and the cochlea are all in communication with each other.   There is also a fluid named perilymph *outside* the membranous labyrinth, that is to say, between the membranous and the osseous labyrinth.   The osseous labyrinth—in shape similar to Figure 33—thus contains first perilymph, then the membranous labyrinth, and within that endolymph.

It is a matter of interest to note the angle at which the ear drum is placed (Figure 32).   The advantage of this provision of Nature is, that a larger surface of membrane is thus exposed to air vibrations than if it had been placed at right angles to the external acoustic meatus. It is said that in the case of certain idiots known as cretins, who are found in some Alpine villages, and also in the case of deaf mutes, the ear-drum is set in a still more oblique position, whilst in musicians the drum is frequently more perpendicular. This is a condition of things that appeals to our sense of reason, for if the ear-drum be set too obliquely it would be less sensitive to the air vibrations, whilst a slightly added perpendicularity would make the drum more sensitive.

There are many other points of interest which could be added, with respect to the anatomy of the ear, but this is probably as much as, and even more than, the ordinary musical student will require. If further information be wanted, it can be found in the medical works already quoted.

<h3 style="text-align:center">K, PAGE 108</h3>

The writer is fully aware that nerve experts state that the power conveyed by the nerves is not electrical, but inasmuch as they do not, and apparently cannot, tell us what it *is*, the term electric energy is used here for want of a better expression, for the term will convey more meaning than the phrase ' excitatory process,' which is frequently used in technical books dealing with the subject.

Dr. W. Biedermann (Extraordinary Professor of Physiology in the German University of Prague) tells us in his book *Electro-Physiology*, that the mode of action within the nerves has often been compared to that of the telegraph system, and so long as we bear in mind that what is transmitted in the nerve is *not* electricity, the comparison is a very fair one.

This explanation is added only for the sake of being exact. The reader will doubtless realize that the energy to which reference is made is simply that power which the nerves convey to the muscles, and the term ' electric current ' will possibly here convey more meaning than ' excitatory process ' or ' electro-motive force.'

The idea first stated in the 1918 edition of this book and continued in the 1922 issue, that the energy conveyed by the nerves to our muscles is distinctly an electric power—and not merely an ' excitatory process '—is now becoming received and adopted. In the *Medical Times* for May 1926, is an article on ' Electric Cell Life ' by O. C. Overbeck, F.R.S.A., F.C.S., in which the following statement occurs : ' We know of no movement whatever anywhere in the whole universe which is not of electronic origin. Movement itself is merely the manifestation of electric energy, and can be produced by no other means.'

<h3 style="text-align:center">L, PAGE 109</h3>

Naturally since 1900 further developments have arisen, the latest in the musical field being the Hammond electric organ. This extraordinary instrument is a practical demonstration of the progress made in the science of controlling frequencies and vibrations for it gives results which would have been thought impossible 15 or 20 years ago. It is now possible to have a cathedral or concert organ which will not go out of tune, without pipes and without reeds or wind pressure. The tone is produced entirely by the controlling and mixing of fundamental pure tones with their relative harmonics and overtones.

M, PAGE 155

It is interesting to note that this same *Essay on the Human Under-standing*—a work which has long been an acknowledged honour to our country—gave such huge offence to many people when it was first published in 1689, that it was proposed at a meeting of the heads of houses of the University of Oxford to censure and discourage the reading of it, and, after various debates among themselves, it was decided that each head of a house should try to prevent it being read in his college.

GLOSSARY

ACOUSTIC—relating to the sense of hearing, or to the doctrine of sounds. Gk. ἀκούω, I hear; ἀκουστικός, adjective.

ANTERIOR—in front, more in front.
Lat. comparative adjective, from ante, before; as in antecedent, ante-diluvian, &c. Cf. poster-ior, infer-ior, super-ior.

ANTRUM—Lat., a cave.

ARACHNOID—like a cobweb.
Gk. ἀράχνη, a spider's web; εἶδος, that which is seen; the shape, form.
-oid as a suffix to adjectives, as arachn-oid, cobweb-like, aryten-oid, cup-like, cric-oid, ring-like, ethm-oid, sieve-like, sphen-oid, wedge-like, thyr-oid, door-like, defines the various shapes, according to the noun to which it is joined, and stands for the Greek εἶδος, i.e., the shape or form, as it appears to the eye.
In making such adjectives into English words, the εἶδ is changed into oid, as in tabl-oid, like a tablet, delt-oid, like a delta, or triangle.

ARYTENOID—like a cup or ladle.
Gk. ἀρύταινα=ἀρυτήρ, a cup or ladle.
Thyro-arytenoid means something in the shape of a cup, with a lid (θύρα) on it. See Thyroid.

BRONCHUS—one of the two bifurcations of the trachea or windpipe. Gk. βρόγχος, windpipe.

BUCCAL—relating to the mouth.
Lat. bucca is strictly the cheek. It., bocca; Span., boca; Fr., bouche.

CANCELLATED—of lattice-work.
Lat. cancellus, a grating.
The Lat. name Cancellarius was the title of the officer who had charge of the records. He was so called because his post was by the cancelli, or lattice-work which screened off the judgment seat in a Roman court.
The E. end of a church was called the chancel because it was screened off from the rest of the building by a cancellus, or grating.
Obliterating a deed was called 'cancelling' it, i.e., drawing lines across it in the form of trellis, or lattice-work:

CARTILAGE—gristle, elastic tissue.
Lat. cartilago, gristle.

CELLULAR—formed of tiny cells, pockets or boxes enclosed in membranous envelopes.
Lat. cellula, a little chamber; diminutive of cella, a storeroom, hence our words 'cell' and 'cellar.'

CICATRICE—the scar of a wound.
Lat. cicatrix, a scar. Cicatricial, adj., connected with a scar, or

produced during the formation of a scar.

CILIA—microscopic hairs in a fringe.

Cilia, plural of Lat. cilium, an eyelid or eyelash. Hence supercilious, disdainful, as expressed by raising the eyebrows; super, above, and cilium, eyelid. French, cil, an eyelash or eyebrow. It., ciglio. Span., ceja. Ciliated, fringed with cilia.

CLAVICLE—the collar bone.

Lat. clavicula, literally, a small key, a tendril of a vine. Diminutive of clavis, a key, which is allied to claudere, to shut.— *Skeat's Dict.*

Clavicular, relating to the collar-bone.

CONSTRICTOR MUSCLE—one which constricts, or draws together.

COSTAL—relating to the ribs.

Lat. costa, a rib, side. Hence, the coast or side of the land. Fr. côte, a rib, sea-coast; and côté, side.

CRANIUM—the skull.

Gk. κρανίον.

Cranial, adj., relating to the cranium, or skull.

CRICOID—like a ring.

Gk. κρίκος, a ring, and εἶδος, a form.

DEFAECATION—the act of purifying from dregs; purification; the act of discharging faeces.

Lat. defaeco.

DIAPHRAGM or MIDRIFF — the membrane which divides the thorax from the abdomen.

Gk. διά, between; φράγνυμι, I enclose.

DIPLOE—the medullary substance or porous part, existing between the plates of the skull.

Gk. διπλόος, double.

EPIGLOTTIS—the cartilage lid at the root of the tongue that covers the wind-pipe during the act of swallowing. Gk. ἐπί, upon; γλῶσσα, tongue.

EPITHELIUM—a thin skin which lines the internal cavities and canals of the body.

ETHMOID—sieve - like, porous, spongy.

Gk. ἠθμός, a strainer, sieve, or colander, and εἶδος, a form.

EXCISED—cut out.

Lat, ex, out; caedere, to cut.

GLAND—a roundish organ occurring in many parts of the body, and, generally, secreting some fluid.

Lat. glans, the acorn, *i.e.*, the dropped, or shed, fruit.

GLOTTIS—the narrow opening at the upper part of the windpipe. It is capable of expansion and contraction.

γλῶττα is the Attic form of the Gk. γλῶσσα, the tongue.

HYDROGEN—literally, the generator of water. The gaseous elementary substance which, with oxygen, combines to form water.

Gk. ὕδωρ, water, and γεν, to produce—the base of γί-γν-ομαι =γι-γεν-ομαι, I am produced or born.—*Skeat's Dict.*

HYPOGLOSSAL—pertaining to the underside of the tongue.

Gk. ὑπό, under; γλῶσσα, the tongue.

Cf. epi-glottis.

INFERIOR—lower in position.

Lat., comparative degree of inferus, low.

Cf. anter-ior, poster-ior, super-ior.

INFUNDIBULUM—a funnel.

Lat. fundo, I pour; in, into.

KINK—a twist or coil in a rope.

A Dutch, Swedish, and German word.

LARYNX—the upper part of the windpipe.

Laryngeal, connected with the larynx.

Laryngectomy, complete removal of larynx.

Laryngoscope, a reflecting contrivance for examining the larynx.

Gk. λάρυγξ, the top of the windpipe ; σκοπέω, I look at, examine.

Cf. telescope, microscope, etc.

LATERAL—related to the side.

Lat. latus, side.

LIGAMENT—a strong, flexible band which binds two or more parts together.

Lat. ligare, to tie.

MANOMETER—an instrument for measuring the elastic force of gas or vapour.

Gk. μανός, rare, thin in consistency, not dense ; μετρόν, a measure.

Manometric, relating to or observed by means of the manometer.

MAXILLARY—belonging to the jaw-bone.

Lat. maxilla, the jaw-bone ; from mala, the cheek-bone—derived from macerare, to chew, macerate.

MEATUS—a passage or duct.

Lat. meo, I go, or pass.

Cf. per-meate, to penetrate, or pass through.

MUCUS—a sticky fluid secreted by the mucous membrane, which it serves to moisten, lubricate, and protect.

Mucous, its adjective—slimy, secreting the mucus.

Mucous membrane is the membrane, or thin skin lining the cavities of the body which open externally, as the mouth, nose.

Gk. μῦκος, only found in Hesychius.

Lat. mungo (obsolete).

Cf. mucilage, gum.

Lat. membrana is the skin covering a member of the body.

NARES—Lat.,nostrils, nose outlets.

NASAL—connected with the nose.

Lat. nasus, the nose. Nozzle, diminutive of nose.

NASO-lachrymal secretion from nose, connected with tears.

NERVES—the whitish, fibrous threads ramifying through the body, whose function is to convey sensation and originate motion.

Gk. νεῦρον, a sinew. Lat. nervus.

NITROGEN—that which produces nitre. Nitrogen is the main ingredient, i.e., about four-fifths, of atmospheric air, the rest being chiefly oxygen.

Gk. νίτρον, and γεν. cf. Hydrogen.

NODE—a knot, or swelling.

Lat. nodus, a knot ; nodulus, dim., a little knot.

OESOPHAGUS—the gullet, or canal through which food and drink pass to the stomach.

The etymology is unknown.

OSSEOUS—bony.

Gk. ὀστέον }
Lat. os, ossis } a bone.

OXYGEN—'A gaseous element which, with nitrogen, forms atmospheric air, and, with hydrogen, forms water.' Means 'generator of acids.' From Gk. ὀξύς, sharp, and γεν, cf. Hydrogen.

PALATE—the roof of the mouth.

See Max Müller's *Lectures*

on Language, 2nd series, 1864 ed., page 252.

PHARYNX—the cavity forming the upper part of the gullet. See Oesophagus.
Gk. φάρυγξ, a chasm or throat. Pharyngeal, its adjective—belonging to or affecting the pharynx.

PHONATION—producing voice or sound.
Gk. φωνή, voice, or sound. As in ' telephone ' : τῆλε, afar ; φωνή, a voice.

PNEUMO-GASTRIC—pertaining to the lungs and stomach.
Gk. πνεῦμα, air or breath. Hence, pneumatic, pneumonia, etc.
Gk. γαστήρ, the stomach.

POSTERIOR—behind.
Lat. post, after.
Adjective : positive—posterus, following ; comparative—posterior, later ; superlative—postremus, last.
Cf. anter-ior, infer-ior, superior.

RE-SONATOR—The prefix re- means ' back,' or ' again,' *i.e.*, repeating. As repeating a blow, or, in this case, a sound, has the effect of intensifying, it is within the scope of ' resonant ' to imply *swelling out* the sound, as is understood by the word ' sonorous.'
Lat. re, back ; sono, I sound.

SEPTUM—a partition.
Lat. sepio, I enclose.
Hence tran(s)sept, a cross enclosure.

SINUS—a cavity, sound box.
Used by Roman geographers to describe a bay of the sea.
Hence our ' sinuous,' winding ; insinu-ate, to wind in and out.

SPHENOID—wedge-shaped.
Gk. σφήν, a wedge ; εἶδος, a form.

STRATIFIED—laid or arranged in layers or courses, or strata.
Hence our ' street.'

SUPERIOR—higher in position.
Lat. preposition super, over.
Adj. positive—superus, high ; comparative—superior, higher ; superlative—supremus, highest.
Cf. anter-ior, infer-ior, poster-ior.

THYROID—one of the cartilages of the larynx, so called because it is like a door.
Gk. θύρα, a door ; εἶδος, a form. In the simpler form thyro, this word is sometimes linked to arytenoid, and then means ' something in the shape of a cup, with a lid on it.'
See Arytenoid.

TIMBRE—the quality distinguishing any tone or sound of one instrument or voice from the same tone or sound of another. Timbre is a French word, derived from the Lat. tympanum, a drum, which we use for the drum of the ear.

TRACHEA—the windpipe.
Gk. τραχύς, rough ; from the rings of gristle which make the pipe corrugated.

TURBINATED—cone-shaped, like a top. Lat. turbo, a top, from the root ter, to whirl, whence come tero, to rub, triturate, and torqueo, to twist, and torques, a twisted necklace.

VALVE—the lid or cover opening or closing a tube.
Lat. valva, the half of a folding or rolling door ; connected with the verb volvo, I roll, which reminds one of the

ancient custom of writing on rolls of papyrus or parchment. Hence our ' Rolls,' or Record Office, and the ' Master of the Rolls.' Hence our word 'volume,' which is, strictly, a roll—from Lat. volvo, I roll, as in ' re-volve.'

VALVULAR—containing valves, or acting as a valve.

VASCULAR—circulation by pipes or tubes, in contradistinction to cellular, which see. Lat. vas, a vessel, from which we get our ' vase.'

VENTRICLES—the two cavities of the heart which propel the blood into the arteries.

VENTRICULAR—relating to the ventricles.

INDEX OF NAMES

N   177

Imaginary Conversations, by W. S. Landor, 40n.
Incorporated Society of Musicians, 21, 164
Institute of Physics, 2
Institution of Electrical Engineers, 109
Integrative Action of the Nervous System, The, by Dr. Charles C. Sherrington, 104n.
Interpretation in Song, by Plunket Greene, 133
Introduction to Science, by Sir J. Arthur Thomson, 48, 49, 61, 95, 113, 133, 152, 155 and n.
'Italian Singing Teaching,' 66

Jackson, Dr. C., 80

'Kaffir War-dances and Modern Music,' by Hubert Bath, 164
Kelvin, Lord, 107
Kennedy, John, 47
Kennedy-Fraser, Mrs., 164
Koch, 158

Lablache, 151
Lamperti, Francesco, 153
Landois, 3
Landor, W. S., 40
Larmor, Sir Joseph, 97
Latson, Dr., 77, 159
Lawrence, Sir Trevor, 4
Learning to Sing, On, 164
Legge, Robin H., 153, 165
Lehmann, Lilli, 51-2
Lehmann, Liza, 151
Life of Lord Lister, by Guy T. Wrench, 165
Light on the Voice Beautiful, by Ernest G. White, 82n., 130n.
Lind, Jenny, 94, 151, 152
Lister, Lord, 55, 90, 153, 157, 160, 165-6
Lives and Letters of Eminent Persons (1813), ed. by John Aubrey, 6n.
Lloyd, Dr. W., 61

Locke, John, 149-50, 154-5, 170
Lodge, Sir Oliver, 111
Lombardia, 66
London Mathematical Society, 97
Longfellow, H. W., 49
Lootens, Charles, 31
Lost Art of Singing, The, by M. A. R. Tuker, 2, 22
Lowell, James Russell, 147
Lunn, Charles, 3n., 4, 32, 37, 50-1, 70n.

Macdonald, Prof., 109, 111
Mackenzie, Sir Morell, 3, 4
Mallinson, Albert, 138, 142
Manual of Voice Training, by E. Davidson Palmer, 52
Marage, Dr., 57, 62
Marconi, G., 1
Marcus Aurelius, 88
Mario, 151
'Market of Voices, The,' by Romeo Carugati, 67
Martels, M., 52
Matthay, Tobias, 13, 23, 43, 125
McLellan, Dr., 41
McNaught, Dr. W. G., 44
Medical Times, The, 169
Melba, Dame N., 126
Mémoire sur le Mécanisme de la Voix pendant le Chant, by M. Bennati, 52
Mikulicz, Dr., 81
Mill, John Stuart, 62
Moore, Thomas, 154
Morning Post, The, 145
Morris, Dr., 116
Mott, Dr. F. W., 61, 62
Moura, Dr., 81
Mozart, 153
Mulford, Prentice, ix, 104 and n., 149 and n.
Müller, Prof. J., 57
Murphy, Agnes, 126
Musical Education and Vocal Culture, by Albert Bach, 42, 43
Musical News, The, 62
Musical Standard, The, 72n., 155

Streeter, Rev. H. B., 95n., 149
Surgical Anatomy, Vol. II, by Dr.
John B. Deaver, 60
Sutro, Emil, 71
Sweet Singer, A, by Agnes
Murphy, 126
System of Operative Surgery, A,
by Dr. W. Douglas Harmer,
80-1
Stuart, Prof. Anderson, 11n.

Taylor, David, 45
Taylor, Jeremy, 121
Tetrazzini, Luisa, 137-8, 153
Text Book of Anatomy, by Dr.
Cunningham, 70, 167n.
*Text Book of Human Physiology,
A*, by Landois and Stirling, 3
Text Book of Microscopic Anatomy,
by Sir Edward Schäfer, 168
Thackeray, W. M., 85
Thomson, William, *see* Lord
Kelvin
Thomson, Sir J. Arthur, 48-9, 61,
95, 113, 133, 135, 152, 155n.
Thomson, Sir St. Clair, 20
Thring, Rev. Godfrey, 140
*Throat and Nose and their Diseases,
The*, by Dr. Lennox Browne,
72 and n., 101n.
Tomes, Sir John, x, 75
Treatise on Anatomy, by Dr.
Morris, 116

Tree, Charles, 74
True Method of Voice Production,
by J. van Brockhoven, 69-70
Tuker, M. A. R., 2, 22
Tupper, 148n.
Turner, Dr. Logan, 34
Tyndall, Prof., 63

Vesalius, 88
Victoria, Queen, 55
Vincent, Florence, 143
Voice, The, by Dr. Aikin, 33, 56,
59-60, 106, 159 and n.3
*Voice Beautiful in Speech and
Song, The*, by Ernest G. White,
97
Voice Building and Tone Placing,
by Dr. Holbrook Curtis, 16, 27,
52, 56
Voice, Song and Speech, by Dr.
L. Browne and E. Behnke,
101 and n.

Wallworth, 22
Watson, Sir William, 132
Webster, William, 80, 107
Whistler, James, 53, 84
Wolcot, Dr. John, 49
Wrench, Guy T., 84n., 165
Wylie, 120
Wireless Telegraphy, 71

Young, Prof. C. A., 33-4

INDEX OF SUBJECT MATTER